LEAVE THE BUILDING QUICKLY

True Stories

CYNTHIA KAPLAN

HARPER ● PERENNIAL

NEW YORK ● LONDON ● TORONTO ● SYDNEY ● NEW DELHI ● AUCKLAND

AUTHOR'S NOTE

Any identity that required protecting has been
protected. Also, that the word "ass" and its
various incarnations seem to appear with alarming
frequency in this book is entirely coincidental.

HARPER ● PERENNIAL

Four essays were originally published in slightly different form in the
following: *Organic Style:* "A Squirrel Stores His Nuts"; *The Worst Noel:*
"Donner Is Dead"; *The Modern Jewish Girl's Guide to Guilt:*

"American Express"; *Talk Softly But Carry a Big Lipstick:*
"Foreign Correspondent."

A hardcover edition of this book was published in 2007 by William
Morrow, an imprint of HarperCollins Publishers.

P.S.™ is a trademark of HarperCollins Publishers.

HarperCollins books may be purchased for educational, business, or
sales promotional use. For information please write: Special Markets
Department, HarperCollins Publishers, 10 East 53rd Street, New
York, NY 10022.

FIRST HARPER PERENNIAL EDITION PUBLISHED 2008.

Designed by Susan Yang

The Library of Congress has catalogued the hardcover edition as follows:

Kaplan, Cynthia.
Leave the building quickly : true stories / Cynthia Kaplan. — 1st ed.
p. cm.
ISBN: 978-0-06-054851-3
ISBN–10: 0-06-054851-7
1. Kaplan, Cynthia—Anecdotes. 2. Entertainers—United States—
Anecdotes. I. Title.

PN2287.K23A3 2007
791.092—dc22   2006047086

ISBN 978-0-06-054852-0 (pbk.)

08   09   10   11   12   ID/RRD   10   9   8   7   6   5   4   3   2   1

"Five things we can't live without this week: 4. *Leave the Building Quickly*. Cynthia Kaplan's entertaining and sometimes touching true-story collection includes recounts of a Disney Cruise from hell and her run-in with a deer, as well as a story about the American Express card she gave her grandmother. Get it." —*Sun-Sentinel* (Florida)

"The author of *Why I'm Like This* continues to detail her life and her observations about the world, religion, love, sex, and whatever else comes into her quirky brain in her second book of 'true stories.' The result is funny, sweet, poignant, and even slightly bawdy at times. The reader will find herself nodding in agreement to many of Kaplan's colorful, situational observations. [*Leave the Building Quickly*] will alternately make you laugh and hit you with a surprisingly strong emotional punch."
—*Cleveland Jewish News*

"Actress and comedian Kaplan's musings on her life are hysterically funny. Her take on sex after childbirth alone is worth the price of the book. But she also reveals phobias, sibling relationships, in-laws, friends, baring her soul as she examines each. She's the woman we would all like to call our best friend—her sense of humor is enough to keep us laughing through the worst of times."
—*The Inkslinger* (Salt Lake City, Utah)

"Kaplan's first book got me through my first few weeks of graduate school, and her second through a recent plane flight. Reading her discussion on fear of flying might not have helped, but then, it might. She writes about things that make you feel self-conscious, like how she and her brother didn't really talk growing up, or how no one kissed her in high school. If you want light, dry, and slightly neurotic, it's all here. Also, read her first one." —Third Place Books

"Kaplan has a gift for recounting stories from her life in a way that will make you snort milk out of your nose. I recently finished reading *Leave the Building Quickly*, her latest collection of laugh-out-loud essays. I particularly liked "Luminol," which re-creates Kaplan's very unfortunate audition for *The Daily Show with Jon Stewart*, and "Very Special Thanks," which spotlights a particularly unhelpful mentor."
—*The Sunday Paper* magazine

"These essays range in topic from smacking a deer with her car, to fat asses, to the existence of God. They are personal and universal at the same time. They are hilarious. And they are beautifully structured."
—A. J. Jacobs, author of *The Know-It-All* and *The Year of Living Biblically*

"Cynthia Kaplan's voice in this wide-ranging collection of essays is infectious. . . . [Her] great gift is making us realize that we've all had dark moments and that it's okay. Her edges are there but softened by humor. She'll tell you anything, and you'd tell her anything too." —*Jewish Book World*

ALSO BY CYNTHIA KAPLAN

Why I'm Like This

For my parents,
whom I hardly blame at all

CONTENTS

This book is not a blessing and it will not heal you. It will not give you hope. If it does give you hope, call me and I'll see what I can do to get rid of it.

All Aboard

By the time I was in college, I viewed family vacations as the thing you did because you weren't in greater demand elsewhere. Being seen with my family at any kind of recreational event was a reminder to me that I had no boyfriend and a dubious social life, or, in later years, was perhaps on the make for a rich widower. I felt simultaneously like a baby and an old maid.

I had friends whose family vacations were like Olympic trials with no drug testing. Their siblings were their best drinking partners, and their parents skied or sailed or whatever with them during the day, but were usually too drunk by cocktail hour to care what their children were up to in the evenings. My parents hardly drank, wouldn't know a wedel from a schuss, and my brother and I had a cordial relationship based upon our mutual disdain for our parents and a shared appreciation for the book *Chariots of the Gods*.

During our middle school years, my brother and I were shipped off on the occasional weekend to the Otis Ridge Ski School in Massachusetts, a frigid purgatory where I spent the entire time trying to avoid the unfortunate fate of the little girl in John Cheever's story "The Hartleys," who gets into a deadly tussle with a rope tow. Guess who wins. Later, during high school, our family made three futile attempts to stage ski vacations. The first was rained out, and the second ended before it began when I contracted mononucleosis, better known as "the kissing disease," a seeming impossibility, due to the fact that nobody had, as far as I could tell, ever kissed me. The last attempt came to an abrupt conclusion when my brother fell and broke his wrist, and my mother, having spent a morning paralyzed with fear on the bunny slope, declared herself "done." Yearly visits to the grandparents in Florida resumed.

It is important to stress that there was nothing inherently wrong with our family. We had loving and involved parents and a comfortable home. Perhaps they were a little too involved, although now that I'm a parent I am convinced there is no such thing. Looking back, it seems the problem with our family was that it offered us too vivid a reflection of ourselves. In my mind, the word "family" somehow evolved into a synonym for "uncool." Neither my brother nor I could have been characterized

during our youth as cool. At our high school, the pin-
nacle of cool was achieved one Halloween by a couple of
jocks who showed up at a costume party with aluminum
pots on their heads. That I myself was at this party was
not in any way a testament to my popularity. I didn't
even know what the guys with the pots on their heads
were supposed to be until someone told me. My senior
year, I had a graduation costume party and two girls
came dressed in all white, each with a drinking straw
sticking straight up from the top of her head. I didn't
know what they were supposed to be and when I was
told, I still didn't get it.

Our parents weren't cool, either. They weren't dorky
or frumpy or embarrassing in any way — they just weren't
cool. In fact, the things that made them great parents —
their generosity, their concern, the fact that they didn't
get too bombed to pick us up from parties on weekends —
were exactly the things that cool parents weren't. Cool
parents let you wear wedgies despite their correlation
to broken ankles, they let you affix those velvet post-
ers of castles to your walls with Scotch tape, and they
had no *idea* where you were at ten o'clock. They were
too absorbed in their own lives to be overly involved in
the details of yours. Perhaps, had my brother and I been
more subversive, perhaps if we'd actually staged surrep-
titious little adventures during our family time, it would
have been redeemed. The most reactionary thing we ever
did was mime to each other across the dinner table the

various forms of suicide, a time-honored diversion which I'm sure still engages thousands of siblings worldwide. I'd pretend to throw back a handful of pills with a gulp of water, and my brother, in response, would mime hanging from a noose. This would continue until we'd exhausted the more farfetched possibilities, such as mixing combustible fluids in invisible beakers and dying of ennui.

Of course, now that my brother and I both have spouses and children, our parents have acquired a new identity. They're still not cool, but that's not a problem, since they are not so much our parents anymore as our children's grandparents. Like our ancestors before us, we have spawned a buffer generation. Although I'd already padded the relationship several years earlier by marrying well. My parents definitely like my husband more than they like me. For one thing, he plays golf with my dad, and for another, he's not a bitch.

Did I just mention my spouse? I believe I did. Did I say that he came with his *own* family? Also true. A family totally unlike mine. A family of avid golfers and skiers, fond of traveling the country together in search of places to avidly golf and ski. They had a vacation home in Vermont and spent a good portion of their winters traveling back and forth between it and Westchester. In one car. When I joined their clan, I suppose I half expected all this madness to stop, in deference to me.

I have actually been on several vacations with my husband's family. My mother-in-law loves her family and she loves to travel. Put the two together and, well, you can just imagine. Wait, you don't have to, because I'll tell you. At the risk of sounding ungrateful, because I'm not—my mother-in-law is one of the most generous people on earth—I dreaded these vacations for weeks, if not months, before they took place. Once again, there is nothing inherently wrong with David's immediate family. They are smart, fun-loving, outdoorsy people and I can't say enough nice things about them, I really can't. And that's because it's not them. It's me. In the three years I saw a therapist we just never got around to family vacations.

The first Froelich family vacation I went on was a trip to a resort masquerading as a ranch in Big Sky, Montana, the summer I was pregnant with John. The posse consisted of David's sister and her husband, his brother and his brother's (one day to be ex) wife, his mother and her gentleman friend, and us. Although if I could have left the fetus here in New York at a utero hotel, like you leave a dog, I would have. Anyway, I woke up one night a couple of weeks before the big trip in a panic. Actually, I woke up almost every night of my pregnancy in a panic, but the subject of this particular panic was germs. I'd been sick on and off for a good part of the pregnancy and had finally seemed to hit an extended off period. As I lay in bed at four in the morning, I conjured in my mind a picture of the Froelich family hiking through Big Sky country in the high-altitude glare of the sweltering Big Sky sun. I, of course, was well prepared with hydration; my personal sherpa, David, was carrying several liters of Poland Spring. As we wound our way skyward—the air thinning, the heat thrumming in waves before our eyes—one by one, David's coughing, sniffling, ill-prepared relations begged for relief. What to do? I imagined their various ailments—TB, avian flu, bubonic plague—and I shook David awake. I made him promise that we would not share any drinks or food with his family. He assured me he understood and would back me up.

Not five minutes from the airport in Bozeman, our merry band stopped for lunch at a little grill. As we sat down with our food, David's mother reached over to help herself to some of his milkshake. I flinched. David looked at me and then at his mother. "Cindy is afraid of getting sick, so we can't share anything with anyone, and that includes you, Mom," he said. I would add *contemptuously*, but that just doesn't do his tone justice. He then rolled his eyes and after that shut them and shook his head. Oh, the shame, the shame. I regarded him coolly and then, after a moment, I turned to the others and said I agreed that I was silly, yes, and neurotic, but I did not think that was as bad as being an asshole. There was agreement all around. David spent the rest of the vacation overzealously guarding my well-being and accomplishing the many meaningless little tasks I devised for him.

And, may I say, what a nice vacation it was, too. The weather was lovely; we had some vigorous hikes on which no one asked me for water; and there were Frosted Flakes at the breakfast buffet. I learned to fly-fish, which was a treat, as each of our river guides was more of a manly man than the next. They didn't say much, but they didn't have to. All they had to do was walk me down the river out of sight of my husband and then help me with my technique. The week flew by.

And then it came to a crashing, flaming wreck of a finale, courtesy of you know who.

At supper on our last night in Big Sky, David's mother, who was, and surely deserved to be, extremely pleased with the success of the vacation, made the charming and generous suggestion that we convene like this *every* year. Naturally, I kicked David under the table. Naturally. And David, still working off that milkshake debacle, opened his big mouth and translated my kick into the King's English. He said something like, "Gee Mom, I don't even take *Cindy* on a vacation every year. I think I'd want to do something alone with her next time. Don't *you*?" Well, I don't think she did, because her face crumpled and she put her head down and began to cry. At that moment, all of the warm summer air was sucked out of the room and in its place blew a chill, chill wind. The rest of the family looked as though they were considering carrying out some kind of lurid cowboy justice. David's mother got up and left the dining room. David and I followed her and lay down on the gravel pathway in front of the building, prostrate with regret. Of course, we should have just said "Thank you" and "Sounds wonderful" and then done what we liked later on. But we—I say we but mean I, because I don't believe David would have said anything unless I'd kicked him—just couldn't bear the thought, the sheer presumptuousness, that we didn't finally, *finally*, have a grown-up life to live and the grown-up vacations that go with it.

Our next full-fledged Froelich family excursion came several years later. Soon after Emma was born, David's mother began concocting her most elaborate plan yet. For her seventy-fifth birthday, she wanted to take her family, grandchildren included, to Mexico during school break. She'd bought a time share at a Mexican resort and had been trying to do something called "banking": she'd been saving up her weeks in order to book them all at the same time.

The idea of Mexico brought about discontented rumbling deep in my bowel. We had been to Mexico just the year before (with David's mother!) and I'd spent the next few weeks processing food at an alarming rate. In fact, I'm one of those people who don't actually have to eat contaminated food for it to wreak gastrointestinal havoc. I just have to hear about it, even from a friend of a friend of a friend. Fortunately, I got the break I was looking for in August, when it appeared that the Mexican scheme was in disarray and would not be arrayed in time for the vacation.

Remember that old saw, "Be careful what you wish for"? The next I heard, David's mother, on the recommendation of one of her bridge buddies, had booked all sixteen of us, yes, that's right, sixteen—all children, spouses, and grandchildren—on a Disney cruise. Frankly, "Disney" and "cruise" were two words I'd never sought to utter on their own and certainly hoped never to use in tandem. I get seasick on most boats unless I'm the one steering, and there wasn't much chance I'd be permitted to steer an ocean liner. Also, I'd long felt that if I went to my grave without having been to Disney World or any of its various incarnations, I could consider myself a success as a mother. But the lessons of Big Sky had not yet been and perhaps never would be forgotten, and when I got on the phone with David's mother I pronounced the prospect of a Disney cruise delightful. Then I promptly erased the conversation from my memory.

As the February break loomed, I became more and more concerned about the approaching embarkation. At the crux of my dismay, *The Poseidon Adventure* aside (although I defy anyone to put it aside), was something called the Norwalk virus. It was a horrible stomach flu–like affair that had struck, or rather struck *down*, hundreds of cruise-ship passengers during the previous year's holiday season. That it was named after a town two towns away from the one where I grew up seemed a sign from the geography gods to abort. Furthermore, when the subject of the vacation week came up among several mothers at morning drop-off at my son's school, it turned out that one woman had in fact taken a family cruise the year before, and she warned me that one of the first activities organized by the crew for the passengers' pleasure is the mandatory lifeboat drill, complete with sirens, ear-shattering horn blasts, and flashing lights. These things I relayed to my husband, late at night, when I couldn't sleep and he appeared to have been, soundly. I started calling the Norwalk virus the Connecticut virus, to make it seem more ominous. I rambled on about rogue waves, a concept I had become familiar with from reading *The Perfect Storm*. After David fell back to sleep, I lay awake thinking about all the vacations I never took and how if I died on this one it would somehow be fused with my identity. *She was on a Disney cruise when it happened.*

As predicted, our first onboard activity took place to the mellifluous tones of the ship's siren. I immediately panicked upon finding only three life vests in our cabin—two adult- and one child-sized. (From now on, when I say *cabin*, what I mean is a wood-paneled closet that sleeps four.) I hoped this shortage of flotation devices wasn't an indication that the Disney Company expected me to choose between my two children. We pushed the button labeled *concierge* on our boat phone and within moments we were equipped with a little blow-up baby skiff. In the event of a real emergency, we were to strap our daughter in and as she floated, screaming, upon the swells, David, John, and I would bob around her, trying to keep the seagulls from pecking at her eyes.

Miraculously—or not—the children remained calm throughout the evacuation rehearsal. I say "or not" because had they (or, for that matter, I) flipped out, it might have provided us an excuse for immediate debarkation, which, indeed, would have been miraculous. When it was over, we put our flotation devices back in the closet in our closet and proceeded to the main deck for the welcoming party, which consisted of ten perky crew members on a stage doing an aerobics routine and lip-synching to "Who Let the Dogs Out." It was during this spectacle, or rather, while trying to avoid this spectacle, that I surveyed the shipscape and became cognizant of the dirty little secret of cruise ships. Or, rather, *secrets.* There are several.

In television commercials, cruise ships look impossibly large, like they might have golf courses on them. The pools appear Olympian in size, and sunbathers are fanned out on the decks as though it were the Italian Riviera in August. When you hear that these vessels are the length of two football fields, it seems as though the outdoor activities are limitless. Maybe there will even be an exhibition football match between the Detroit Lions and the Miami Dolphins. Once onboard, however, you realize what the Disney Company means by "Magic Kingdom." On our ship, it had achieved a sort of magical inversion of space, where one's perception of the available exterior space was incorrect in the exact inverse proportion to one's ability to comprehend the enormity of the interior space.

The interior of a cruise ship is like a hotel lobby in a nightmare. It is comprised entirely of elevator banks and miles of hallways carpeted with ocean-motif carpeting, which ultimately lead to doors that say *Ladies* and *Gents.* It is impossible to know from one moment to the next what deck you are on or whether you are fore or aft. Within the nine or ten stories of public space there are two enormous restaurants that sit one atop the other and, except for the décor, are exact replicas of each other; a nightclub; two theaters, one for movies and one for "Broadway-style productions"; several kids' clubs, although why you'd travel to the Caribbean so your child can play video games and watch Disney shorts *indoors*, I don't know; and, finally, various three-story atria providing space for the ongoing pantomime of live Disney characters, the lines of children waiting to be photographed with them, and the parents and grandparents waiting to photograph the children being photographed. Grand, winding staircases bracket each atrium (I still do not know how many such spaces there were—three, ten?) like parentheses. You go up one and down another and the next thing you know you are a half-hour walk back to the restaurant where you were having dinner.

There are three pools on the ship's main deck. Three! One is the size of a lap pool, one the size of a largish Jacuzzi, and the last, the children's pool, is the exact size necessary to ensure that every time a child jumps in, he or she will land on another child's head. This pool has a two-story slide, the line for which snakes around the deck like the line outside the Limelight. There are always fruit and ice cream and pizza and hot dogs available—hey, it's not a spa vacation—and fruit smoothies.

According to the ship's itinerary, we were to spend one day and night traveling south on the high seas, dock at Nassau in the Bahamas, then travel again overnight to Disney's own private island for a beach day, and finally motor on back to Florida. For those of you out there interested in such an excursion, here is some advice I'd like to give you before you zip up your suitcase. Pack some sweats or something and maybe a wool cap. The weather on the deck is often cold and windy. While the ship is moving from one port to another, being outside is like being in that bug-spray commercial where the people put a jet engine–size fan in their home to keep the bugs from landing on them. They wear goggles to protect their eyes, in order to walk they clutch a clothesline, and when they talk they must shout.

And don't watch the cruise commercials that show women in bikini tops and sarongs sipping piña coladas as they lean over the railing and gaze out at the open sea. Watch any movie from the 1930s or 1940s—people are always standing around in overcoats or are lying on long wood-slatted chaises, scarves slapping furiously at their faces while white-gloved stewards tuck blankets around their legs.

Here's perhaps the dirtiest little secret of all. *You are never alone.* One of the lines my mother-in-law used when pitching the trip to the rest of the family was fed to her by the friend who'd suggested the cruise. The woman had said something to the effect that the ship is so enormous that you never see another soul. I can tell you that this is absolutely true if you close your eyes. The ship we were on can accommodate 2,600 souls. I think the breakdown was 1,600 passengers to 1,000 crew members, give or take a few souls. To Disney's credit, they run a tight ship, the crew are helpful and courteous, the service is swift and comprehensive. Furthermore, the place is spotless and the food's okay. But who wants to vacation with 2,600 people?

And guess what happens when the ship docks at Castaway Cay, Disney's private island, and you disembark for a day at the beach? So do the other 2,599 people! You all trek or trolley to the beach, where you lay towel-to-towel and swim shoulder-to-shoulder, like one big happy family. Some stroke of luck led us back to the boat early, perhaps it was a sprinkling of rain, perhaps it was the lack of available space in the ocean, but oh, what joy we discovered upon our return. The ship was, for the first time, virtually empty. We snagged some front-row chaises at the kids' pool and while Emma slept in her stroller, John took five hundred turns on the two-story slide.

There was more, but in case you are planning your own Disney cruise, I don't want to spoil all the surprises. Well, maybe just one. On the final night of the cruise, the ship sailed the open seas to thrilling effect. Contrary to my mother-in-law's theory that "the boat is so big you don't feel anything," we were tossed about our beds on a kind of *Little Mermaid*–meets–*Titanic* amusement-park ride. The boat swayed and bucked, rose up and crashed down. The wood paneling creaked and groaned and strained, sounding as if the entire ship were preparing to implode. I was sure, on a frequency just below the din, I could hear Emma rolling hither and thither in her crib, like a silver ball in a pinball machine. I made David get up and wedge John into his little daybed with pillows, so he would not end up folded upon himself on the one square foot of available floor space. In the pitch dark, with no horizon on the horizon, I was both horribly seasick and petrified. I prayed not to die, or rather, to die just for a little while, just for the night.

I know that there are people for whom a Disney cruise, or *any* cruise, would be the vacation of a lifetime. To them I say, cruise away, and I encourage them to love every minute of it. I myself am not sure I will ever recover from mine. If it is possible to be both agoraphobic and claustrophobic at the same time, then I would say that that pretty much sums up my experience. That and the fact that still, in my little, little mind, a family vacation represents the antithesis of cool, and a family vacation that takes place on a cruise adds insult to injury, and a family vacation that takes place on a *Disney* cruise, well, you might as well just slap some mouse ears on my head and set me atop a homecoming float. You know, the funny thing is that I'm not particularly (or at all) cool now and I don't feel the need for a cool vacation. I believe I can state categorically that I will never be seen on the beach at Mustique, wherever that is, although I said that about a Disney cruise and look where it got me. But I still can't quite shake the feeling that I was there because there were no better offers. It doesn't matter that my husband was there, or that we actually managed to have sex once, which was certainly one more time than I ever had sex on any of my own family vacations. In that vein, I suppose, besides being grateful for my mother-in-law's generosity, for the camaraderie of my brothers- and sisters-in-law, and for our general good fortune, I should just be happy that it was their family on that cruise and not mine.

Ballads of Rusty Magee

I first met my friend Rusty in the summer of 1990, when I agreed to be in an evening of improvisational I-don't-remember-what organized by an actress we both knew at a theater on the fifth floor of a derelict building on Theater Row. This was the kind of thing we used to agree to do. I had just started doing stand-up, or my version of it, which included stories and original songs, and, inexplicably, finger puppets.

Rusty was a composer and occasional actor but was best known for his performances in comedy clubs and theaters, where, seated at a piano, he parodied popular musicians and musical styles. He mercilessly lampooned the music of Jim Steinman, best known as Meat Loaf's songwriter, and the high, hiccupping singing voice of Cat Stevens, whose "Father and Son" he sang without most of the consonants. He sang a tender and funny lament

ce of the LP, the long-playing record
most, perhaps, the loss of the double
pot-sifting properties. He did a sort
ibute to the children's classic *Rusty in
Orchestraville*, which was funny mostly because Rusty
himself bore a frightening resemblance to a cartoon
drawing on the front of the album of a large-headed child
with beady blue eyes, a maniacal grin, and a mop of red
hair, seated at a piano. He often told the song-story of
his alter ego, Rasta Magee, for which he would don a
dreadlock wig and Jiffy Pop hat. He had an excellent
bit about a popular musical lick (a term musicians use to
describe a catchy chord arrangement), in which he basically proved that "Papa Don't Preach," "Kiss on Your
List," "She's So Fine," "Steal Away," "Hungry Heart,"
and the entire Doobie Brothers canon are all the same
song.

What was so brilliant about the way Rusty made fun
of these and other hit songs was that he got you to laugh
at them without making you feel bad for maybe once
having liked them. Because it is not uncommon for songs
to be stupid and good at the same time. When people go
to comedy shows, they want to nod their heads in recog-
nition almost as much as they want to laugh.

Or maybe more. The first time I shared the stage at
a comedy gig with Rusty, he sang Van Morrison's hit
"Brown Eyed Girl" as a sort of encore. He made me stand
next to him at the piano and sing along, and the whole

time I was thinking, *What's so funny?* Granted, Rusty had a particular gift for singing covers. But he would use them for his own purposes. He'd often make faces at odd lyrics or ham up pretentious chord arrangements or key changes. Or he would squeeze in extra words, commenting on his mood or something in the audience or current events. But "Brown Eyed Girl" got special treatment, because nothing Rusty did to it changed the fact that it is a great song, a jolly, contagious song with a chorus so good that if you don't smile while you are singing it someone should notify your next of kin that you're dead.

Hey, where did we go, days when the rains came? What an opener! I don't know about you but *I'd* like to remember a time when there was a *we* and we had a place to *go*, if you know what I mean, when it rained. Well, it turns out we went down to the hollow and slipped and slid in the morning mist, we took a transistor radio down to the old mine, we did all sorts of excellent things. Van Morrison describes a youthful love so bright and shin-ing, so carefree—who wouldn't want to remember that or something like it? Now, of course, some of us won't remember it because it never happened, but we love to hear those lyrics anyway so, for a moment, we can *pre-tend* that it happened. We can *imagine* what it was like "making love in the green grass behind the stadium." Sort of. If we hadn't been virgins at the time.

Great songs elevate our own pedestrian yearnings to

not only a place where they rhyme, but to a place that is filled with other yearners, singing along, making us feel less pedestrian. For Rusty's audience, singing "Sha la la la la la la la la la la dee da" was the magical incantation of the romantic ideal that we conjure in adolescence and which informs, in some way or another, every romantic encounter of our lives. Rusty sang as though the song had happened to him, and the reason we sang along was because it could have happened to all of us. It should have happened to all of us. Maybe it still would.

Why did Rusty do it? If you think about it, for him to transition from comedy about music to music for its own sake during a comedy show, without the whole enterprise turning to cheese, was nothing less than astonishing. Really ballsy. Maybe he just thought, *Hey, I've got the stage, I'm going to sing whatever I like.* But maybe it was this: Rusty knew that laughing in the dark with two hundred total strangers feels great, but *singing* with them, well, that feels *fantastic.* In the Celebrity Deathmatch between comedy and music, music wins. Comedy stars are not and never will be rock stars. Sure, comedy makes you happy, but music makes you happy *and* sad *and* often makes it more likely that you are going to get laid. And when Rusty actually invited you, yes, YOU, out there in the audience, to join in, it was as though the funniest, most popular kid in school had linked his elbow with yours, like Mickey Rooney in *Babes in Arms,* and marched you through the corridors, singing at the top of his lungs, proclaiming his allegiance. It was like you were pals with the guy who had dated the brown-eyed girl. Over the years it became standard for Rusty to end his comedy set with "Brown Eyed Girl." The audience expected it, craved it, and it sort of turned him into a rock star.

Rusty became sick in the fall of 2000. He'd been suffering from colitis since he was a teenager, and although Rusty and I had been performing at the same gigs for more than ten years, colitis isn't among the funnier ailments, and he hadn't ever mentioned it. I went to visit him in the hospital and the first thing he said to me was, "Shit, isn't this insane? They have no idea what's going on." His wife, Alison, an actress and singer who was rehearsing a new musical out of town, flew home. His preteen son, Nat, went to stay with friends. There was an operation, and the doctors found a malignant tumor at the top of his colon. I went back to the hospital after the surgery and Rusty was in utter shock. "Shit, I have *cancer*. Shit. Can you believe it? *Cancer*."

During Rusty's first round of chemo, in the winter of 2001, a song called "Drops of Jupiter" was getting that kind of new-song radio play that happens once in a while, particularly with mid-tempo rock ballads. I've always thought that the rock ballad was a particularly potent musical form. Rock music has the rhythm of a heart beating just a little bit too fast. Pump it up and it's all adrenaline rush, slow it down and it's pure emotion. Play something in between, and you can dance and cry at the same time. It doesn't even matter that most rock ballads are about lost love only a little more often than they are about dogs.

Also, there's nothing like fantasizing about heart-heavy rock stars, even if they're freaks. I mean, who wouldn't fuck Kiss drummer Peter Criss, cat whiskers and all, after hearing him sing "Beth?"

"Drops of Jupiter," by a band called Train, is, ostensibly (I say *ostensibly* because some of it is so incomprehensible I couldn't really tell you what it's about), a sort of postmortem inquiry into the nature of the afterlife. Its lyrics imagine what it might be like to be, how to put this, "out there," in the heavens, floating around, discovering new worlds, missing old ones. (I read on a music blog that the singer wrote it just after his mother had died, which redeems it a bit. I'm a mother.) "Drops of Jupiter" is both driving and a little drecky, a combination that is one of the hallmarks of a successful rock ballad, and, true to form, it's chockablock with hackneyed clichés and baffling metaphors. My favorite is "She listens like spring and she talks like June." Oh, wait, no, this is my favorite: "Told a story about a man who was too afraid to fly so he never did land." Although, who am I to sneer, since (1) the CD went double platinum, and (2) I myself have an utterly inexplicable attachment to the song "Total Eclipse of the Heart."

These are just the kind of lyrics that would never have survived a once-over by Rusty. He would have stopped short after singing this stunner, "She checks out Mozart while she does Tae Bo," and asked "What the fuck?" and then sang on with the same pained, incredulous face he always made when he sang the Jim Steinman lyric—perhaps his stupidest ever—"Objects in the rearview mirror may appear closer than they are." Actually, stupid and *dangerous*, because the opposite is true. Objects in the rearview mirror are *closer* than they appear. I'm wondering how many Meat Loaf fans failed their driving tests.

Rusty played "Drops of Jupiter" for me three times in a row one day, without irony, picking out particular lyrics, singing along, manically pacing his living room, sitting down at his keyboard and getting up again—for someone on chemo he had a lot of energy. He played it for everyone. He talked about it. He obsessed over it. So, how do you go from being a "Brown Eyed Girl" kind of guy to a "Drops of Jupiter" kind of guy?

You get cancer. You get cancer and you see your life, which was perfectly represented by Van Morrison, suddenly turn into something that is better represented by Train.

So what if Rusty didn't bother to parse the lyrics too carefully? He just let himself be swept away by the alchemy from which hit songs are somehow born of inane writing, a catchy melody, a driving beat, and, perhaps more important, *coincidence*. In the opening stanza there's a totally nonsensical line about acting like summer and walking like rain but it ends with the suggestion that it is not too late to change. That first part about the summer and the rain, yikes, but the second half, well, *everyone* wants to change. *Everyone* wants to know there is still time to do it. Especially someone for whom time has suddenly become an issue. Here's how the chorus ends: "And did you miss me while you were looking for yourself out there." Clunky, yes, but it boils down to this: someone went away and someone was left behind. It only takes one or two lyric lines, one or two lyric lines that seem to be about *you*.

As Rusty got sicker, friends from every stage of his life, from every school he'd ever attended, every show for which he'd composed music, every comedy club in which he'd performed, began showing up in his hospital room, at his apartment, visiting with him, taking him on errands. Colleagues and co-writers and ex-girlfriends (some with brown eyes, some with blue) flew in to see him perform and to pay tribute to him. It was nothing less than a pilgrimage. What was it about Rusty? One of his best friends called it "the disarming spectacle of sheer joy." Another said, "Rusty isn't really a grown man's name." And it occurred to me that perhaps Rusty played "Brown Eyed Girl" because it was a reflection of the way he saw his life: a mostly elegant, occasionally messy confluence of nostalgia and hope. Nostalgia and hope. They are the admixture of great songwriting. And they are also, in many ways, the cornerstones of our emotional lives. *Here's where we were; here's where we're maybe going. If we're lucky.* The brown-eyed girl in the Van Morrison song wasn't a *her*, she wasn't a memory, or, rather, she wasn't *just* a memory, she was a *you*, which implied that maybe she was standing right there, in front of Van Morrison, and he was talking to her, and who knows where things could go from there? But Rusty was probably not going to be running into any more metaphorical brown-eyed girls. He needed a new paradigm, and "Drops of Jupiter" comforted him with its implication of a celestial afterlife, especially one in which it might be possible to come to terms with his loss, and then, perhaps, return as some benevolent antimatter to witness his family's recovery through a hole in the troposphere. Nostalgia and hope; even Train got it right.

As with all things musical, Rusty knew what he was doing.

Look, I don't know how to tie this up neatly. Or I'm afraid I'll tie it up too neatly. Let me force an end by saying that once I knew this fantastic, talented guy who loved comedy and music, shared them with everyone he knew and a lot of people he didn't, and then lost his life. Go spend $17.95, or whatever, to buy any Van Morrison

CD with "Brown Eyed Girl" on it—it's something you should own—and one day, after you've blown half an hour peeling the cellophane off of the CD case, play the thing. It's all there. Then buy "Drops of Jupiter" from iTunes for 99¢ and listen to that too. And imagine Rusty. Or someone you once knew. Then go back to "Brown Eyed Girl" and sing "Sha la la la la la la la la la la dee da." Because Rusty would have wanted you to. And because it will make you feel really, really good.

A Squirrel Stores His Nuts

Once upon a time, long, long ago, when my husband was not my husband but my boyfriend, he would buy me porn for Valentine's Day. Every year, come February 14, I'd open a four-by-seven-and-a-half-inch package to find nothing fancy, no lingerie or chocolates or jewelry, just the $3.99 special from the video place around the corner from his office. *Gypsy Queen.* That may have been the first one. A girl is saved from the clutches of her overly affectionate uncles by a gypsy youth who then brings her to meet his caravan. There were other titles too, like *Love Potion #5* (we had not seen 1–4), *Bonnie and Clyde: Outlaws of Love* (this isn't the same as the one with Warren Beatty and Faye Dunaway), and *The House on Chasey Lane*, my favorite, not because it was the best video, but because it starred an "actress" called Chasey Lain and I perceived there to be a pun in the title. I didn't read anything into David's choice of videos; it was probably fairly random. He couldn't have spent more than a couple of minutes in the store. But, as they say, it was the thought that counted. We had to turn them off, though, when we actually wanted to have sex, because watching them inspired a running critique a la *Mystery Science Theater 3000*.

Life was good.

So it came to pass that we got married and had children. And, like all the other things in David's life that didn't change—his job, his basketball game, his yearly boys' weekend in Vermont, his *life*—neither did his sex drive. Why should it? In fact, it may have increased, given that during the years I carried and nursed our children I had breasts the size of half-cantaloupes. With this in mind, and as we were expecting our second child and having hormone-induced sex all the time, I advised him to store up some good sex memories. Like a squirrel stores nuts, I told him, for the long metaphorical winter of the child's first year, during which I would surely have no interest in him whatsoever. The hormones that made me want to have sex almost nightly when I was pregnant were bound, once the baby arrived, to depart. And once they were gone, I would not want to have sex, not even with Eddie Vedder, were that an option.

It is ironic, isn't it, that men witness their wives grow these truly resplendent breasts and at the same time are expressly forbidden to touch them? Well, it cannot be helped. Nature did not intend women to suckle both children and grown men simultaneously. No woman who is nursing full-time feels like having her nipples teased or licked or rubbed or even looked at by anyone who does not measure his age in months. And any man who thinks that a woman wants to stick *anything* up the same opening that just expelled a seven-pound organism, should try it himself, up his opening, such as it is, and see how much he enjoys it.

But I have to say, in the months following the births of our children, the issue wasn't just sex. I had a concurrent lack of interest in the broader, more philosophical notion of a husband as well. Father, yes, sure—the kids need a father, and theirs has proved to be an excellent one—but I found myself serenely disengaged from his everyday comings and goings, except with regard to (1) my childcare needs and (2) when we might have dinner, because I was usually starving by six.

Then, one day, not long after Emma was born, I happened to come across a short article in a ski magazine about a woman who had three children and a husband with a very demanding, high-powered job. The piece quoted her as saying something like she didn't bother her husband with any of the details of child-rearing or housekeeping, because after ten years of marriage she wanted him to continue to think of her as his girlfriend. It seemed that she even tackled home-repair jobs on her own. My first thought was, *Wow, I'm such a bitch.* My next thought was: *Is there something to this?*

Before anyone gets angry, I'm going to answer that question. No. Okay? No. As far as I'm concerned, David can take what he gets and like it. I am reminded of the various years in my twenties, when I went without sex, because there seemed to be nobody good to have it with, and, you know, it wasn't so bad. The loneliness was worse. So, I didn't feel that sorry for David; life's rough all over. At least he had me and the kids.

Sure, I'm tough, but I've got to be. Conventional wisdom and your ob-gyn consider breast-feeding to be a sort of contraceptive. Both because a woman often stops menstruating while breast-feeding and because the super–love hormones released during this time are aimed at the child, not the spouse. However, I have another theory. The defensive wall erected by breast-feeding hormones against the husband/aggressor is an act of self-preservation on the part of the new mother. I think many women—and if by many women I mean just me, that's fine—need time to orient themselves to the fact that the world as they have known it has been jettisoned off orbit and into the cosmos, perhaps never to return. While they have happily satisfied their longing for a child—I personally longed good and hard—they have likely sacrificed not only their work but the often thrilling sense of being unencumbered, of freedom and self-determination that existed before. That they have done this knowingly, even willingly, does not change the very fact of it.

Which gets me to wondering just who the ski-magazine woman was before she was a wife/mother/handyman/sex toy. (Whenever I picture her now in my mind, and I do, it is in a tank top, shorty-short cutoffs, and a tool belt.) Did she have a profession or a dream of one? Or perhaps this is who she always was, a high school sweetheart who got laid in the back of a Chevy Impala parked at the town beach, was handy around the house, and helped raise her siblings. And if she is content with her choices now, more power to her. I didn't really need to read about it, but still, more power to her.

Here's who *I* was, though. I was this actress/free-spiritish (emphasis on the ish) person. By the time I met David, I had agents and worked all the time for very little money and was friends with many other equally busy if still obscure actors. I already had a life. A life I had studied for and trained for. A life I unequivocally felt I belonged in. But it wouldn't have mattered what I did. I could have been anything, really, a doctor or a lawyer or a French-to-English translator at the U.N. The point is that it was *my* life.

This is not to say that I didn't want a family. I did. I wanted it *too*.

No one ever said I couldn't have both. David certainly didn't. But somehow, when push came to shove — that is, when our son was born — something changed in me. My desire to act wasn't diminished but rather I seemed to lose the ability to organize the day in my head, a result, perhaps, of some fatal amalgam of fervent mother-love, breast-feeding, exhaustion, and guilt. I still squeezed in a little work here and there, which made me simultaneously ecstatic and despairing, because the life that went with the work, its daily rhythms, its open-endedness, was gone. I love my children ferociously, but there are moments when I feel crushed by the loss and furious at David, who for all intents and purposes appears to have gotten off scot-free.

Some people say sex becomes more intense for them after they have children. They cry when they orgasm and are almost afraid to look one another in the eye, *it's all so much.* Sex changed for me, too, not because of what I gained, but because of what I lost. Being an actress was a key part of my identity. It was who I'd wanted to be my entire life, before I ever wanted to be a wife or a mother. It was who I *said* I was, not only to others but to myself. Sex occurs because of an understanding between two people about who they are—man/wife, jock/cheerleader, Lord of the Manor/upstairs maid. The person I was used to being, the person I *liked* being when I had sex, seemed to have disappeared. I felt simultaneously bereft and also strangely embarrassed, as though my credibility had been materially damaged. This may sound like an ancillary emotion, but it rocked my ego almost completely off its mooring, and as a disincentive to sex, it trumped many times over the argument about being too pooped from a day with the kids.

I will admit that after the birth of our daughter I tried holding off sexual relations for a while with the occasional hand job. At one point, after about four months, I had to ask David if we'd had sex yet. I actually couldn't remember. (My ob-gyn says that an Alzheimer's-like loss of memory occurs during the period when a woman is breast-feeding her child. It's just one more thing. Whatever.) If, in some twisted, near-psychotic way, between feeding my child and *struggling for my very survival,* I wanted my husband to pay for the fact that having children was, for the most part, a simple addition equation for him, not the complex calculus that it was for me, then so be it. So he suffered for a while. I did not feel then that I could add live-in slut to his bounty.

But he's no dummy. That year he returned from his boys' weekend in Vermont with two gifts. The first was a skimpy halter top. I wore it at dinner with friends, and right before dessert he whispered to me, "You look twenty-five." The second gift was a video with a priceless title: *Dirty Fucking Skanks.* When I saw that, I laughed out loud. It didn't mean that I'd made my peace with him (and when I say him, I mean me) or that I would *ever* be the mother/maid/girlfriend I read about in the ski magazine, but that night he got laid.

I can't tell you what other people feel or do, how they reconcile themselves to the losses they incur when they stop working or the ones they worry they have imposed upon their children by continuing to do so. And I'm sure some people want to have sex all the time no matter what's on their minds. I only know what I've felt and done, mostly because I couldn't help myself, because it was both human nature and my nature, and because my husband showed no inclination to be a house-husband. But I am scrappy—that is also my nature—and when my children get a little older, when I feel they need me just a little bit less, I will pick up the (sad violin music here) broken shards of my former identity. Or I'll sweep them away. Or better yet, it is my hope, no, my expectation, that in the near to middling future my old self and my new one will agree to some sort of time-share arrange-ment, where they take turns inhabiting the space of my life, such as it is now, and take turns, as well, having sex with my husband.

Losing My Religion

For as long as I can remember, I believed in God on airplanes. I prayed as the plane took off and I prayed as it landed. I prayed through turbulence and recently I said a quick Shema after becoming aware while taxiing on the runway that there was a swarthy man with disturbing facial tics sitting directly behind me and my daughter. I thought perhaps he was nervous about something, like the bomb in his shoe, but David said it looked like a neurological condition, so we didn't disembark.

This is how I used my faith. Insurance-policy Judaism.

In synagogue, I recited along with the rest of the congregants in a full, hearty voice; what an excellent opportunity to practice the stage standard pronunciation I'd learned in acting school! I sang all the songs I knew and hummed the ones I didn't or sang nonsense lyrics, which is sort of what Hebrew sounds like anyway.

When I stood for the mourners' Kaddish I did my best to appear mournful, and when I sat through the silent prayer I was silent. I dressed in wool on Rosh Hashanah no matter how summery the weather, and I brought brown-paper grocery bags full of food for the hungry on Yom Kippur, which seemed like a reasonable request, whomever it came from. My lack of sincere devotion to these rites was a reflection of a sort of noncommittal agnosticism. You could say I was agnostic about being agnostic. When I was growing up, my parents never referred to God or called upon Him or quoted His spokespeople—you know, Moses, Jesus, Muhammad, Joseph Smith, whomever—unless you count "goddammit!" or "Jesus Christ!" No one in my family ever uttered the words "God will provide" or "the Good Lord willing" or even "Oh, Lordy." There was never any talk of mysterious ways or divine intervention. As far as the liturgy went, at our religious-school confirmation, my friend Ellen and I played our guitars and sang the song "Where Are You Going?" from the musical *Godspell.*

A couple of years ago, however, I stopped praying in synagogue. At first I couldn't quite put my finger on what happened. I suddenly found myself unable to participate in all the God talk. Now, I like Reform Judaism. If I could choose from all the world's religions, I would choose it again, I like it so much. I like that we're not supposed to take everything literally and that arguing is not only allowed but encouraged. I like the bagels and lox and I like that my grandmothers called me Cindeluh. But here is what I think happened. I think it dawned on me, slowly, without my even quite knowing it, that I could not, in good faith, so to speak, reconcile any idea of God with the current state of our world. There have been many scholarly attempts to do just this since the dawn of time, from the Book of Job to *When Bad Things Happen to Good People*, but every explanation, as far as I can discern, inevitably answers questions regarding logistics by telling you it's still about faith, which is where you started in the first place and why you had all those questions.

So, this notion had been creeping up on me for some time, uneasily flopping around on the sofa of my subconscious, trying to either get comfortable or just get up and leave. Then, one night, following a dinner of Thai food and ice cream with peanut-butter-cup mix-ins, I sat with my husband and our friends in the dark of a movie theater and, by the time the credits rolled, I had come, once and for all, to the conclusion that there is no God.

What was the movie, you ask? No, it was not *Showgirls*. Nor was it Mel Gibson's *The Passion of the Christ*. (Raise your hand if you thought the ambush of Jesus in the Garden of Gethsemane looked like outtakes from *The Blair Witch Project*.) Nor was it *Snakes on a Plane*.

It was *Hotel Rwanda*.

I'd like to say that I never thought I was the kind of person whose entire belief system was based upon docudrama, but there it is. *Hotel Rwanda* = There is no God. Q.E.D.

Why *Hotel Rwanda,* you might ask. What the heck was I thinking when, say, *Schindler's List* came out? (That is, besides what a dreamboat Ralph Fiennes was, even as a Nazi-fatty nut job.) While I was moved to tears by *Schindler's List,* I was already well educated on the subject of the Holocaust, and it was deeply entwined with my Jewish education. If the Holocaust had not shaken the faith of the Jews, why should it shake mine? The fact is that there have been many, many fine Holocaust movies and war movies and movies about real-life affliction so immense that it would seem impossible that the events these movies portrayed managed to evade God's watchful eye. And yet we believe. And not only did God often appear to be A.W.O.L. from films depicting past human catastrophes but from films predicting future ones as well. Should we believe in a benevolent God who sees fit to spare only Dakota Fanning and Tom Cruise? Well, we do.

Obviously, I'm not talking about movies, really. (Well, I sort of am. Though I am loath to admit it, there are things I've learned in a dark movie theater that I did not know about before, and one of them involved Marlon Brando with a stick of butter.) I'm talking about human tragedy on a scale inconceivable to most of us, to me, who lives comfortably in New York City and has food to eat and clothes to wear and is not in immediate peril, as far as I can tell, from twisters, insurgents, or famine. And although 9/11 may well have been but a portent of horrors to come, I cannot appropriate it for any purpose here. I am, for now, safe and warm and free, and I am as far removed from the holocausts of my own lifetime as I am from those of the past. Why should I be susceptible to *Hotel Rwanda*? What took me so long? Perhaps I missed a *Frontline* back in 1994 or something; had I not, I might have forsook the possibility of God's existence ten years sooner. But the idea of God wasn't relevant to me back then, and, shamefully, neither were the people of Rwanda. There it is. In 1994 my beloved Florida grandmother died, my father had a heart attack, and my boyfriend asked me to marry him. It was a time of manic depression, and it is entirely possible that I didn't read anything but the Arts section of the *Times* for a year.

So, what happened in Rwanda, anyway? I can believe one maniac with a machete, maybe a few soldiers, but a whole population? Why didn't the Hutu, for example, say, "Dismember my neighbors? Hmm, that doesn't sound very nice. I think I'll pass." What, exactly, is the point of a god who commands all these things — don't kill, don't hate, don't steal blah blah blah — and people do it anyway, in droves, and then go to church or synagogue or mosque and get on their knees. Obviously nobody's listening. Or rather, someone will declare it "God's word" and who can argue with that? Only an atheist. God's poor name is used and abused so often, in order to justify such atrocities, that what can a person believe except that Man is not His servant but that God is Man's. We made Him up to explain everything that was inexplicable and defend everything that was indefensible.

How else to account for the Mormon fundamentalists? Although, I suppose, were I a man and invited to join a religion based largely upon the precept that I should take multiple wives and populate the earth with my resulting abundant spawn, I might just ask where to put my John Hancock. It's not a bad proposal. Of course, the revelation stipulating polygamy arrived just around the time Mormon founder Joseph Smith decided he wanted to cheat on his wife, but why nitpick?

Okay, that was an easy target. Yet this is the modus operandi of virtually all fundamentalist movements, whatever religion they are sprung from. They instill in their followers a belief in their moral, and sometimes intellectual and physical superiority, in their chosen-ness, if you will. They convince them that their edicts are directives from God, which is how religious and political leaders through the ages have gotten their flocks to do their bidding, finance their empires, wage their wars. Besides that, there are few stronger incentives than worrying that when the day of reckoning comes you are going to burn in hell. Maybe it's better to just go along? Is there any other way to explain Rwanda? Or, for that matter, Bosnia and Somalia and Chechnya and the current calamities that are Iraq and Darfur?

And what about George W. Bush, the Hebrew National hot dog of presidents, answerable only to a higher power? The results of a recent poll, reported by the *Winston-Salem Journal*, says that one in five Americans believe that God is on the side of America when it comes to world affairs. *One in five.* A professor of sociology of religion, who helped devise the survey questions, said the results show that "the idea of God, the belief in God, can be in a political sense exploited for nationalist purposes, at least for that fifth of the country. In that sense it's an important finding." Important? No, *terrifying.*

In some kind of weird coincidence, I received an e-mail from a dear friend, with the words "There is a God" in the subject line. For two hours, I didn't open the link she provided, because I was sure it was a computer virus. What a brilliant lure; who doesn't want to know that God exists? But my curiosity got the better of me, and I ended up watching a video clip from the CBS evening news about an autistic boy from a small Midwestern high school, who had become, through hard work and fierce determination, the manager of his school's boys' basketball team. It seems like he mostly helped out at practices and was the water/towel boy at games. Well, in the last game of the season the coach suited him up so that he could experience some of the excitement of sitting on the bench as a real team member. And then in the last few minutes of the game, the coach put him in. The kid scored twenty points in like four minutes, most of them fantastic three-pointers. His team and the crowd went berserk, and when the buzzer sounded they carried him off on their shoulders.

It's a *great* story. *Great.* I'm sure it will become a movie. But here's my question. What's this got to do with God? It seems to me that it has to do with a kid who loves basketball and a bunch of terrifically generous, spirited human beings with big hearts and open minds. Why can't we give them the credit they deserve? Maybe they're all atheists, who knows? Why is God watching over this autistic child, gracing him with this, I don't know, basketball glory, and yet we don't hand Him the responsibility for Darfur or the debacle that is the Bush-Cheney administration? Why aren't we just mad that there are all these autistic children? Why does God get all of the credit and none of the blame? We blame the bad men and we praise God for our ultimate deliverance. Why the delay? Maybe we should stop waiting for God to deliver us, and deliver ourselves.

One day, while I should have been writing or playing with my children or opposing global warming, I was flipping around the TV and found myself watching the opening minutes of the talk show *The View*. The subject up for discussion was intelligent design, a concept, I believe, disseminated by the religious right to further enthrall the people of our country in their power. I, personally, have always believed first and foremost in science. I have never put any stock in the Creation or the afterlife or ghosts or reincarnation or souls flying up from bodies. I think that Dionne Warwick is full of shit. I don't even like her voice. Not that science and faith are mutually exclusive; my father's cousin Gerry was a devout Jew as well as part of the team of scientists who developed vitamin C tablets and L-dopa. Anyway, Meredith Vieira and Joy Behar, the smarties, were firmly positioned against intelligent design, while Star Jones and the younger one—whose name I had previously denied entry to my memory port (I have just now looked it up on the Web and identified her as Elisabeth Hasselbeck)—came down on the side of *who's to say?* Which, on its face, is fine. Who *is* to say? However, Hasselbeck seemed to have developed a sort of ratings system against which things of beauty were to be measured in order to determine if God was involved in their creation. In this way she concluded that Michelangelo *definitely* must have had some help from God. I can only assume that ferrets had none. Star Jones, a woman of some intelligence, I believe, stated her unshakeable belief in evolution with the following caveat: when she looks into the innocent eyes of a newborn, she knows that only God could have created that.

What's with the cherry-picking? God did this, God

didn't do that. Everyone is going to have a different opinion of what God hath wrought. The authors of the Bible did. (Hey, they wrote the Bible!) In having such an opinion, *we* define God, not the other way around. How else to account for the many different gods? We each have the god we want, the god we need. Who, besides Mel Gibson, is to say what's true?

In *The Thirteen Clocks* by James Thurber, there is an invisible character called Listen, a spy whom everyone both reveres and fears until it is revealed at the end that Listen is actually the imaginary construct of another character, a sort of magical little man called the Golux, who says, "Never trust a spy you cannot see."

Or, to put it another way, and while I'm on the subject of daytime television: a very long time ago, I was home watching *The Joan Rivers Show*. This was when she still looked like Joan Rivers and not a member of Jocelyn Wildenstein's inner circle, or should I say, pride. Joan's first guest was a woman who claimed to have been living in a house that was haunted by the disgruntled spirits of some earlier occupants. She described in fairly graphic detail how they had been abusing her and, in fact, sodomizing her on a regular basis. In one instance, she had run screaming down her street, fully clothed and in broad daylight, while a horrible apparition was attached to her from the back in the worst possible way imaginable.

"You mean he was actually sodomizing you while

you were running down the street?" Joan asked. "My God, that must have been terrible."

"It was," the guest replied.

In the past, when I have found myself in the occasional theological discussion (haven't we all?), I have described myself as a Buber-ish Jew, a reference to Martin Buber's *I and Thou*, which I read my senior year of high school. Bringing up Buber has always been an excellent way of skirting a conversation about God. Believe me, no one picks up the thread. The reason being that Buber is unintelligible. You have to read every sentence five times as though translating it from another language, sort of like *The Sound and the Fury* — how else to figure out which Quentin Faulkner's talking about? I'm no rocket scientist, but I was a conscientious student and had the patience to read things five times, especially if my grade depended on it. Anyway, I recently rejoiced to find that there is a new translation of *I and Thou*, slightly less unintelligible than its predecessor and, best of all, it comes with an excellent, lucid prologue by the translator, which may (and, at times, did) preclude an in-depth rereading of the most inscrutable portions of the text, which means most of it.

Buber's basic premise, in a nutshell, if I may be so bold as to venture that it fits in one, is that God is found in our humanity. That is, our relationships with each other. Buber believed that God is present in what he called the

I-Thou relationship. Or I-You, in the most recent translation, which makes more sense, because Thou sounds
like it refers to God, which it doesn't; it refers to another human being: *you.* Anyway, Buber's message was
sort of a theological extension of E. M. Forster's famous
"only connect." If we can't communicate reasonably and
meaningfully with our fellow human beings—that is, as
opposed to, say, hacking them to death with a machete,
or gassing them, or blowing them up—then we haven't
a *chance* of communicating with God. We cannot coexist
while viewing each other as alien life-forms or inanimate
objects or existential mistakes God made while casting
about for His *real* chosen people, i.e., us. We must see
ourselves in each other. On Christmas day in 1914, British and German troops stopped shooting at each other,
called out "Merry Christmas," swapped food and ciga-
rettes, and played soccer. There was a very good book
about it, and even a movie with Ethan Hawke. To me,
this is what Buber meant. If there is a portal to God, this
is where to find it. I am sure that this concept is at the
bedrock of all great religions but that everyone has just
sort of conveniently forgotten it. A friend once said to
me that she tries to behave *as if* God exists. That's okay
with me, but I believe that the difference between good
and evil is apparent, and if we cannot figure it out ourselves, then whether God exists or not is moot.

Strangely enough, in the process of losing God, and
besides the fact that I'm worried I won't be able to stop

saying things like "Oh, my God" or "for God's sake," I have found myself to be newly attracted to some of the more practical aspects of Judaism, the most compelling of which is that we do not believe in the afterlife. We are responsible for the life we are in now. This also means that we are responsible to each other first, with God a close second. This notion is perfectly manifested during the holy day of Yom Kippur. At the very beginning of the Yom Kippur service, the rabbi asks the entire congregation for its forgiveness. He admits that he may not have been as helpful, as patient, as understanding as we may have needed him to be. He tells us that he is deeply sorry, and that in the next year he will try to do better. The rabbi says this every year and I am always moved. Then he reminds us that we all must ask forgiveness directly from those we have harmed; it's not enough to ask God. Of course, later we'll apologize to God, *a lot,* but for now this is just between us mortals. To me, Yom Kippur is sort of like a mini-funeral in another religion. It is as though the afterlife is just the next year, and we continue, during our lifetime, to try to earn our way into it by being good to each other. In Judaism, unless you are decorating your home with furniture from Seaman's, there is no buy now, pay later.

I was at a benefit for a humanitarian organization, and a student who had been working with this organization abroad spoke about meeting Paul Rusesabagina, the hotel manager whose amazing and courageous story is depicted in *Hotel Rwanda.* The student asked him why, when he had the chance to flee Rwanda with his family in the days before the Hutus descended upon his hotel, did he remain. He said he sat his family down and told them that yes, if he left he would be able to live with them for many years to come, but he would not be able to live with himself.

I understand that it is easier not to shoulder the entire load alone. Just because I am a God-less heathen doesn't mean I don't respect the great potential the belief in God has to buoy people who are floundering and to unite people who are disconnected. If the conviction that God is there with you gets you through the day, rock on. It is, surely, a wonderful thing to feel that we have help, that we can be saved. And religion can be a worthwhile umbrella organization for people who want to make sandwiches for the homeless and send warm coats to children who don't have them. A learned friend has suggested to me that organized religion is a lot like American democracy. It's not perfect, but it's a lot better than anything else anyone has come up with to inspire people to unite for the sake of the common good. I buy that. But it can be lethally dangerous as well. In his astonishing book *We Wish to Inform You That Tomorrow We Will Be Killed with Our Families,* Philip Gourevitch writes that in the earliest days of the Rwandan genocide, Hutu Adventist pastors collaborated with the Hutu Power parties by luring their Tutsi congregants to gather for safety in their churches and town halls, and then stood by while they were massacred. In one town, Mugonero, a final plea for protection from hundreds of petrified Tutsis to the president of the local church (*and* a pastor himself) was met with the following response: "God no longer wants you."

I don't know if Paul Rusesabagina believes in God, but perhaps, were I to meet him, I would ask.

Ah, anyway, so what? If I don't believe that God chiseled the Ten Commandments with a lightning bolt and cured Ben Hur's mother and sister of leprosy, so what? Who cares what I believe? Who's asking? No one. Not even my children. John currently worships at the altar of the Hulk ("He's not a bad *man*, Mom, he just does bad *things*.") and Emma is an iconoclast—she addresses her father as "you big baboon."

I just wish we could all agree that religion is a shared belief in the same story, plus hope, plus some guidelines for decent behavior, and leave it at that. Or, to quote the writer Anne Lamott who, by the way, happens to be a *huge* fan of Jesus: "You do what you can, what good people have always done: you bring thirsty people water, you share your food, you try to help the homeless find shelter, you stand up for the underdog."

That learned friend I mentioned, upon reading the above, has suggested to me that I have written myself in a circle of sorts, and that one might conclude from my essay that I do, in fact, believe in God—a Reform, Buberish version—but God nevertheless. My response to this is that if God is the new name for the collective ideal, that's fine, and if religious people, whether Jewish or Catholic or Episcopalian or Muslim, want to call what is best in us God or Jesus or Allah or L. Ron, I'm jiggy with that, too.

Perhaps it's just semantics, but I, personally, can't call it God. Too much water under the bridge. I'm going to need to come up with some other word. In the meantime, I offer this credo to live by: Believe what you want to believe and don't be an asshole. I mean, how hard could that be?

Donner Is Dead

A deer hit us. We were driving along, minding our own business, when a deer jumped out of the woods, or maybe it jumped out of another car, who knows, and ran smack into us. We were on Route 7 driving north, about five minutes out of Bennington, on our way to celebrate A Jew's Christmas in Vermont.

Christmas is just lovely in Vermont. Really, all the lights and the wreaths and the snow-tipped steeples. You can light candles every night for a year and shake groggers until Haman rises from the dead, but Hanukkah isn't fooling anyone. It's a diversionary tactic, kind of a "hey, over here" that Jewish parents employ to keep their children from feeling like those toys that get shipped out to the Island of Misfit Toys in *Rudolph the Red-Nosed Reindeer*. Everyone claims that Hanukkah isn't meant to compete with Christmas. "It's a festival, it's a festival!!!" No one even knows when the hell it is. It changes every year. I'm not sure the *Farmer's Almanac* could predict it correctly.

Anyway, we didn't see it coming. All of a sudden, there was a very loud thunk, and then what seemed like a two-hundred-pound snowball exploded up and over the front windshield. My husband yelled, "What the fuck?" and I yelled, "Fuck!"

We pulled over to the shoulder and sat for a moment in silence, trying to make sense of what just happened. It was a clear, bright night and very, very cold, maybe ten degrees. The air was thin; you could see for half a mile. There'd been nothing in the road. "I hope that was a deer," said David. "What else could it have been?" I asked. "I don't know," he said, "a person?"

David called the Bennington police and then, with some difficulty, because the door only seemed able to open about ten inches, he got out of the car and walked around the front. Through the windshield, which, thankfully, was still there, I saw him mouth, "Holy shit." He squeezed back into the car and said that the driver's-side headlight was gone and the whole front left of the car was smashed in. The snowball effect we experienced must have been the glass from the headlight shooting up like sparks in the dark. The driver's-side mirror was gone. David thought he saw some deer fur stuck to the ragged metal. Thank God.

There were police lights up ahead. A patrol car passed

us by about two hundred yards, crossed the median, and came to a halt. The police were going to check on the deer first.

Here's what I don't understand: Why didn't natural selection work for the deer? Cars have been around for what, over one hundred years, right? Why haven't the stupidest deer died out? Why hasn't the gene that tells a deer to cross a four-lane highway become obsolete? Why aren't the smart deer at home in their beds making more smart deer?

What's wrong with the deer, I ask you? Zebras have stripes, for God's sake, giraffes have long necks. The leopards that survive in snowy climes are *white*. Was this an accident? No! The white leopards outlived the orangey ones because they were harder to see! And they made more white leopards and now, now, we have something called, yes, the *snow leopard*.

Where is the evolved deer? Haven't we waited long enough? They've certainly turned *tick-carrying* into a cottage industry. *That* didn't take long. Where is the deer that has a natural aversion to headlights? The deer who doesn't like the clickety-clacking noise its hoofs make on the asphalt? Where is the deer that doesn't like the way it feels to lie dying in the middle of the road, wondering what the fuck just happened? Where is he? You know where? In the middle of the road wondering what the fuck just happened, that's where. And while we're asking, what's on the other side that's so important to see at eleven o'clock at night? Better woods?

While we waited for the police, we discussed the fate of the deer. Was it dead? Was it mortally injured? Was there a driver's-side mirror protruding from its head, like an extra set of antlers? The police took so long with the deer we imagined they must have found it alive and were either setting its legs in plaster of Paris or delivering the final death blow. No shots were fired, so perhaps they were wringing its neck.

Our son woke up. Thankfully, his little sister slept on. She would not have been pleased to be sitting on the side of the road at eleven o'clock at night still strapped into her infernal five-point harness. John wanted to know why we'd stopped. Were we in Vermont? he asked. He has finally begun to grasp that Vermont is not just a 1960s faux Swiss chalet with orange shag carpeting and a sectional couch, but a whole landmass, with other houses and trees and people. We told him about the deer, making the distinction that the deer hit us, not we it. If John were a few years older and had a bit of U.S. history under his belt, he might have said something impudent about how the deer were there first, like the Native Americans. Having been absolved of blame, however, he could afford to be magnanimous; he forgave the deer, proclaiming it didn't mean to hit us and "crack" our car, that it was an "accident," and that the deer was probably sorry. Yes, I said. The deer was sorry. Very sorry.

When the police got to us, there were four of them, all without coats. They examined the car and made recommendations about how to proceed with our insurance company. In the fall and winter months this must be their main activity—cleaning deer viscera off the highway and advising motorists on their reimbursement options. Of course, there was a hearty round of thanks that no one was hurt, not counting the deer. There have been more tragic outcomes and we knew we were blessed. Our airbags did not even deploy. It was a Christmas miracle.

The policemen went back to their cars to write an accident report, and one returned about five minutes later with a copy for us. When he handed it to David through the window, he told us in a hushed voice to be careful when we got in and out of the left side of the car, because deer feces were splattered all over it. It's not uncommon, said the policeman.

Huh. So the deer took a crap on our car. I suppose this is some sort of natural phenomenon. The bowels releasing their contents in the midst of a trauma. I feel like I've heard that humans do this as well, in one of the final stages of the death process. But from the deer it felt like an insult, a parting shot, revenge. *You killed me, so I shat on you.* How'd he do it so fast, though? He was going one way, we were going the other, at, say, sixty-five miles an hour. It's not like we saw him mouthing "Fuck you" through the driver's-side window as he flipped past. How is it possible he clung to the car long enough to take a shit and we didn't see him? It's like one of those mind-numbing calculus problems, the ones about the birds flying at different speeds over different distances and you have to figure out how the yellow-breasted pip-pledecker got to Cincinnati first.

We got up and skied the next day, driving our cracked, deer-fouled car to the mountain and back. After yelling "Don't touch the car" at the kids about forty times, David finally took it to a do-it-yourself car wash in Manchester. The day after Christmas, we returned to Manhattan — at night, in a blinding snowstorm, with one headlight and no driver's-side mirror, flouting Darwin.

When we got home, I thought a great deal about the deer we'd killed. John thought about it, too. He had created a spectacular narrative of the accident, such as he knew it, editing and polishing it in order to present it at school during the first morning meeting after the break: "We were driving so so so fast, faster than all the cars, but not as fast as a cheetah. Cheetahs are not the fastest animals on earth. They are the fastest *land* animals. Then Santa was flying infinity-high in the sky and his sleigh was going so so so fast. Then two deer fell off and fell on our car and SMASH. Just like this SMASH. But they didn't do it on purpose. Why would they hit us on purpose? It was an accident." How the Santa thing got in there I've no idea. We may not be the most observant Jews but we definitely draw the line at Santa. I also don't know where the second deer came from. Very grassy knoll.

I couldn't get over the fact that we'd killed something as large as a deer. Not that we kill a lot of small animals. Well, once, driving home from college in a rainstorm, I hit a duck. And we do kill a good number of flies. It is something of an alternative sport in Vermont, like snowshoeing. During the winter months, the flies that live in ski houses become cryogenically paralyzed. When we show up and turn on the heat, they sort of half revive and flop listlessly around the white sand–sprayed ceiling, like stoned beach bums. David walks around with the flyswatter and John follows with a 1975 Electrolux. I suppose, if I were a true animal-rights activist, I would not make a distinction between the value of the life of a deer and that of a fly. But I'm not.

Really, what is it those deer are thinking when they are standing like statues by the side of the road, ready to spring forward to their deaths? What's on their minds? Why can't the deer get with the program? Hey, if you don't like the cars, get out of New England. I'm not particularly fond of research except as a tool of procrastination, but I felt I needed to know why deer were so obtuse. There must be some fundamental, scientific basis for their inability to adapt to the industrial age. I went to the library and let me tell you, there's a *dearth* of literature on the subject. It's pathetic. In the *Eye Wonder* series, of which we are particularly fond, the deer rate a quarter of a page in the book dedicated to The Forest. Our only other option was the book version of Disney's *Bambi*, not the most reliable source of serious information. Then it came to me — *Bambi! Not* the Disney version but the original 1928 novel by Felix Salton. I read it in seventh-grade English and I remember I was deeply moved, deeply. So, I got it out of my library and spent an afternoon rereading it.

Now, I'm sure the story of Bambi is familiar to most. Bambi is a deer born in a forest glade on a warm summer day. He becomes friends with most of the other forest animals — various birds, squirrels, etc. — and a few other deer. Unlike the animated movie, however, this *Bambi* was not meant for small children. I'm not sure it was really meant for *any* children. The deer are at the mercy of the hunter, whom they refer to as Him, and first Bambi's mother and then many of his friends are shot and killed. Around Christmas, everyone being on vacation and all, there is something of an all-forest massacre.

What strikes me most about the novel now is how stupid the deer appear to be. Their conversation is inane, they seem to be ruled entirely by a mixture of confusing urges, and they are unable to identify distinct emotions or separate them from their polar opposites.

They are both terrified and titillated at the same time. They either stand frozen or run completely amok. Their sense of smell is sharp but their memories are vague. They wander off mid-conversation. The words "I don't understand" follow their every utterance, action, or emotion. They're dumb as posts. All the other animals in the forest remark upon their stupidity. Even the squirrels.

Furthermore, their fathers neither live with them nor acknowledge their paternity. Bambi does not know that the old stag who eventually saves his life is his father until the stag is on his own deathbed. As soon as Bambi is able to fend for himself, his mother begins disappearing for days, even weeks at a time, probably off following the stags around, hoping for a little action. After what seems like a months-long absence, she returns for a visit and is killed while leading Bambi across a field. Bambi's cousin Gobo, who has always been weaker than his peers, collapses while trying to escape a hunting expedition and is rescued by the hunter himself, taken home, and made a domestic pet. When he is released into the wild again, he displays no memory of previous horrors. He spends his days bragging about the food that appeared regularly in his little deer dish and the pleasures of life among the fraternity of farm animals and dogs. One day he prances out into the open meadow and is promptly shot to death.

Finally, of all things, Bambi falls in love with Faline, Gobo's sister. Faline is Bambi's first cousin. Perhaps this is why natural selection has failed with the deer. Instead of marrying up, they reproduce with their own, equally stupid relatives, honing their genetic material to a half a helix, or something, and creating generations upon generations of car-chasing dolts who seem particularly fond of leading their families and friends across four-lane highways. If lemmings are the People's Temple of the animal kingdom (drink the Kool-Aid, drink the Kool-Aid), deer are the Heaven's Gate (it's okay, you just need some Nikes and a plastic bag and you're good to go). Sure, I've dashed across a busy city street against the light, but I always, *always* look both ways, and never, *ever* with my kids. All things being equal, although no things really are, the deer seem to have gotten themselves into a dangerous groove. I don't know what it will take to get them out of it. Higher fences? Stricter penalties? Genetic counseling?

Don't get me wrong. I have a deep and abiding esteem for the members of the animal kingdom. That they have survived at all in a world populated by the cruelest of creatures, i.e., Man, is miraculous. I feel neither good nor superior about the death of that deer. It was tragic. And, in fact, I myself do stupid things all the time. Why, just last week I drove home from Vermont with my family in a blinding snowstorm with one headlight and no driver's-side mirror. I'm lucky to be alive.

American Express

About four or five years ago, I got my grandmother an American Express card that was attached to my account. This was, in my opinion, the coup de maître, the master-stroke, of what had become, over time, a veritable catalog of lifestyle "improvements" I'd attempted to impose upon her in her late eighties. At that time, she was beginning to show symptoms of what I at first presumed to be a garden-variety, age-appropriate forgetfulness, but turned out to be the onset of Alzheimer's. While I'd had limited success with some earlier catalog entries — hearing aids, sneakers, and, my personal favorite, non-stick pans — I felt confident that an American Express card was the perfect antidote to her growing confusion during shopping expeditions. Now she wouldn't have to worry about counting cash or writing out checks. She could buy anything she wanted, anywhere she wanted, with The Card, and she could just pay me back later. It seemed like such a reasonable idea, especially since I knew she wasn't the type to stay up till all hours ordering a year's supply of Victoria Principal beauty aids from the Home Shopping Network, or suddenly decide one morning, while cooking Cream of Wheat, that what she could really use was a $10,000 Garland stove.

Up until then, the only credit card she ever had was a B. Altman's card. When it came time to pay a bill, she went to the store and hand-delivered her payment, in full. I'm not sure my grandmother even waited for the B. Altman's bill to arrive in the mail before she took the bus back across town to the store to pay it. In fact, this was how she paid all of her bills. Once a month, we walked her rent check to the rental office of her building complex. The telephone bill was brought to an AT&T storefront on Eighth Avenue.

Maybe she just didn't trust the United States Postal Service, which was odd, because there was a view from my grandparents' window of the old post office on Twenty-ninth Street. A very long time ago, when we were young and short, my brother and I used to stand on the two-foot-high radiator cover beneath the window in the den and watch the postal trucks navigate the rooftop parking lot on the federal building next door to it. It all seemed on the up and up. But these were the Nixon years, and perhaps my grandmother, a former socialist, felt particularly disenfranchised.

When she paid in cash, my grandmother withdrew any one of several combinations of bills and coins from her billfold, her change purse, an inside pocket of her pocketbook, and a second, smaller billfold. Occasionally, she pressed into service the extra twenty she kept in the pocket of her skirt.

The American Express card never quite caught on. Primarily, it turned out that its Enormous Buying Power, such as I was able to describe it to her, was antithetical to my grandmother's sense of privacy. Who needed someone to know so much about you? Where you shop, what you buy, how much credit you have? My grandmother didn't like anyone to know *anything* about her. A person could ask the most innocuous question—where she grew up or if she'd ever traveled to Norway—and she would say later, "What does she need to know that for?" and, indignantly, "She asked me if I'd ever been to Norway! Can you imagine?" My grandmother read judgment into personal questions, as if they were rather questions on a quiz and there was a right and a wrong answer. A wrong answer might mean she was provincial. A right answer might reveal she was too bourgeois. So, my grandmother would say, "Oh, I've been here and there." Her tone would have been coy, but her intent clear. She may well have danced the tarantella with Henrik Ibsen on a moonlit night in Oslo, but if she had, it was no one's business but her own.

I can see now, too, that the American Express card

was too open-ended for my grandmother, its functionality so wide-ranging as to render it irredeemably vague. Who exactly was American Express, anyway? Wasn't it a travel agency? At one point, she asked me if we were going on a trip. I should have dropped the whole enterprise then and there. My grandmother had always been literal-minded, even before the Alzheimer's. Moreover, in her prime, with all her faculties intact, it would never have occurred to her to buy things she could not pay for with the money she had in the bank. Buying on credit was too precarious, too fraught with the possibility of blowing it all, all the gains, all the sweat and struggle. It was even, perhaps, a little unsavory. Where were you going to get this money, anyway, when it came time to pay the piper? Nobody wanted their knees broken. My grandparents lived in the same two-bedroom apartment for over forty years. It was neat and clean and very comfortable, but not too fancy, nothing bought on an installment plan. Besides, fancy was dangerous. Fancy meant that it was always possible that the socialists would come one day, revoke your membership, and occupy your apartment in the name of The People, as they did Ralph Richardson's mansion in *Dr. Zhivago*.

My grandmother's B. Altman's card was more a symbol of customer loyalty than an expression of financial free will. It was a permanent record of her proud affiliation with the store, which may be why she carried it long after B. Altman's closed. It remained in her wallet like an I.D. card. In a way, it was. Altman's sold quality clothes, well made, not flashy, and of good value. That's what my grandmother wore. That is who she was: well made, not flashy, good value.

My grandmother grew up in Russia in poverty. She rarely spoke of her childhood, but I have gathered, from the little she has told me, that her father was the great love of her life. (That is, aside from *my* father. I'm sure she loved my grandfather, too; they were married for sixty-seven years, but, well, *twin beds.*) My grandmother's father was a feckless fellow, not much of a breadwinner but, by her account, merry and charming. My grandmother was the eldest of four girls and he treated her as though she was his son, which, in the old days, was a great compliment. He took her everywhere, often on his shoulders. Maybe that last part isn't true. But it's a visual image I have of them now, jaunty and quixotic, extrapolated from what my grandmother told me, or maybe just from a look on her face. Her father became ill and died when she was nine or ten. After that, the family burned the furniture for firewood. Or something like that. Then the revolution came and they got out. They sailed from Constantinople to Marseille to Ellis Island when my grandmother was sixteen. At least she said she was, so she could work. When she got to Ellis Island, she went into the ladies washroom, took all of her clothes off, washed herself and the clothes in the sink, and then put the clothes back on. That's what they mean when they say they had only the clothes on their backs.

I go to the nursing home today as I have done innumerable times. As I exit the elevator, I see through the giant fish tank that makes up most of the wall between the hallway and the rec room that it is TV time. Rows and rows of wavy figures seated in wavy wheelchairs face a large TV screen. Through the oxygenated, undulating water it looks like an impressionist painting, blurry and vivid at the same time. "The Old and Infirm in the Evening at Westchester." I'm not sure what they are watching; it is probably a rerun of *Matlock* or *Murder, She Wrote*. I don't know why but I wish it was something incongruous, like World Cup soccer. It sure isn't PBS, which is too bad; my grandmother was a lifelong supporter of Channel Thirteen. She drank her lukewarm coffee from its mugs and carried her book-club books and rubber rain-shoes in its canvas tote bags. During her last year in the apartment, she had become an ardent fan of *Riverdance*.

From the doorway, it is not hard for me to spot the back of my grandmother's little white head and bent neck. Even if she was dressed in a Santa Claus outfit and sitting in a sea of Santa Clauses, I would still recognize her from behind. Isn't it funny how that is? Once I would have been happy to find her so situated, in the company of others, but now I am saddened. The old Grandma would never have willingly joined in any such gathering. She would have wandered around on her sturdy, ankle-less legs, doing her own thing, chatting up the desk nurses with her nonsense, snidely refusing to partake in group functions. Sometimes I am sorry my grandmother never swore. She would have been well served by the expression "Fuck that shit."

Tonight she is wearing an outfit I do not recognize. It consists of a white blouse and a faded-to-white floral-print thing that is wrapped around her waist, and I can't tell if it is supposed to be a skirt or what. These items are not hers. Sometimes it still amazes me that I know every single piece of her clothing. Underneath all this is a thin white layer that appears to be a full slip. My grand-mother dabs her nostril with a corner of the skirt. It is not totally unreasonable to believe that she might have mistaken this for a hanky. I am sure she first searched for a pocket in which she hoped to find a Kleenex, be-cause that is where she always kept one or two, neatly folded, along with her key, which was safety-pinned to the pocket lining. I come up to her and touch her shoul-ders. Hi Grandma, I say. It's Cindy. Who, who? she asks. I put my face right up to hers. It's Cindy. Who? Oh, my Cindy. I wheel her away to the winter garden to look out at the falling leaves.

Once, not so long ago, my grandmother, a dressmaker by trade who expertly sewed many of her own clothes, would have as soon wiped her nose on her skirt as she would have sent a holiday card to Ronald Reagan. She took enormous pride in her appearance — her smooth, ironed blouses and soft cardigan sweaters, her fully lined wool skirts with their neat on-seam pockets. My grandfather once told me that one very warm evening, not long after he first met my grandmother, he ran into her at a concert in Philadelphia's Fairmont Park, and my grandmother pretended not to know him. So, partway through the concert, when he found her sitting on a bench with an open book in her lap, he suggested to her that she had brought the book along so people would think she was an intellectual. He told her he doubted that she had even read it. Insulted, my grandmother stomped away, but it was so hot out that her white skirt stuck to her thighs and she had to peel it away in full view of my grandfather. I like to imagine that perhaps this was why, for as long as I knew her, even through dementia, she never wore a skirt without a lining or a slip.

My grandmother also took pride in her hard-earned accomplishments, her spotless apartment with its all-over, moss-colored carpeting and clean white walls, painted every two years. Over time, the light switches had become harder and harder to locate, obscured beneath fifteen layers of Benjamin Moore China White. When my grandmother first saw the tiny, charming brownstone apartment I lived in when I was single, with its hardwood floors and wall of exposed brick, she was appalled. She knew from experience that that was how the poor lived. Certainly, it's where the pogroms, should they return, would find you huddled, perhaps in the pitiable glare of a bare lightbulb. Nice people, people whose grandmothers had B. Altman's cards, for example, had rugs and paint.

We are told that sometimes now she is found sleeping in other patients' beds. And they in hers. Her bras disappear on a weekly basis; occasionally it is clear that she is not wearing one. Among the pictures on her bureau is one of a little girl none of us know. I call her Missy. I like to imagine her to be the sister my grandmother referred to when the Alzheimer's got her to thinking I had one. The photo album of our *actual* family, the one I made for her a few weeks after she moved to the nursing home, has long since disappeared, and I fear some other resident, one with a milder case of dementia, will look through the photographs and gasp in horror because, for the first time, *she does not recognize her own family*.

At first, we railed against the system. My mother sewed name tags into my grandmother's clothes, as she had into mine and my brother's when we left for sleepaway camp. (She probably just snipped a bunch of KAPLANs from what was left of the thirty-year-old roll of CINDY KAPLANs.) So, where are my grandmother's things? Sometimes I worry that people are dying in clothes labeled KAPLAN, an unsettling notion. We demand an accounting of the garment situation from the social worker. She has none. Or, rather, the answer is obvious. My grandmother's fashion sense is a thing of the past. Perhaps the more unrecognizable she is to me, the easier it will be.

She has also become too frail to be taken out of the nursing home. Nothing pleased my grandmother more than getting into our car for the five-minute ride to the local diner. The food there was very mediocre, which was exactly how she liked it. She was ecstatic just to see the car pull in at lunchtime to pick her up and was equally thrilled after the meal when we walked from the diner to the parking lot. It was as though she hadn't seen the very same car in years, much less an hour and a half. She praised it lavishly. "That's a beautiful car you have." Or "Oh, my goodness, that's your car? Since when?" It was there at the diner that, with a supernatural power often attributed in the movies to the aged or to four-year-old Victorian-era children previously thought to have been drowned, she intuited I was pregnant. One winter day, as we waited for David to pay the bill, and apropos of nothing, my grandmother smiled and patted my stomach. "Ahh," she said, and "Well, well, well."

There was a long time during which I felt that I could not have a child as long as I was helping to take care of my grandmother, because, in a sense, she was my child. Then she went into the home and I had a son. It is the natural order of things. The king is dead, long live the king. But so have I been usurped. She loves the baby, *loves* him, but she hasn't said my name unprompted in a long time. I have begun to miss her, the old Grandma, as she once was. I have thought all along that the baby filled the space, but I see now that it is a different space. She and I used to hold hands all the time, even while we were sitting around. "I just need *you*," she would say, clutching my hand, holding it to her cheek. I have stopped holding her hands, because, well, because now I am holding the baby. But is there anything in the world that feels or looks like an old person's skin? The baby's? No, not the baby's. The baby's skin is opaque, it is made up of layers and layers of constantly multiplying cells, it is all promise. My grandmother's skin is transparent, blue-tinged and smooth like something worn down to its essence, like sea glass. It may not withstand the tides another year. Soon it will disappear.

Sometimes days go by now and I don't think of her.

Suddenly, American Express promotional offers are coming to my apartment addressed to Dorothy Kaplan. Does she want to join my gym and get a half-price facial? Is she interested in European travel excursions? Does she want to shop at Michael C. Fina or stay in a Hilton Hotel for a special price if she uses The Card? I'd like to know where they were when she *had* the card.

I'd also like to know why they are not offering any of these discounts to me, when *I* have been a Loyal Card Member Since 1985. Perhaps some small cog in the American Express marketing wheel has been digging up obsolete records in order to fill a quota. The first time it happened, I was startled. No, shocked. Seeing her name like that—it was as if I had received a piece of mail addressed to Rip Van Winkle. But at the same time, I secretly thought: Hmm, Dorothy Kaplan, why, she's, well, huh, these are not concerns of mine anymore. Oh, the relief, now that she was in the home. Which is a terrible thing to feel, I know. But with her safely under lock and key, I no longer had to worry that she would become lost in a blizzard or fall in the bath or leave the stove on. And her chores, how they had eaten big chunks of my days. I certainly didn't miss shopping for her groceries, doing her laundry, sorting her mail into its various categories—junk mail, bills I would pay with her checkbook, things my father should look at when he comes, letters addressed to my deceased grandfather. All that relief was fleeting, however, because sometimes it seemed as though each letter, each postcard that arrived addressed to her was an admonishment, and posed the burning question: *What have you done with Dorothy Kaplan?*

I wrote for a newspaper about the terrible day we put my grandmother in the nursing home. After the piece ran, letters came to the newspaper, some addressed to

the editors, some to me, an almost unanimous outpour-
ing of sympathy. Many people just wrote because they
wanted someone with whom they could share their own
agonizing stories. I was sent e-mails and letters from
around the country, books on Alzheimer's by their authors, and even a tape of Alzheimer's-inspired music.
What that kind of music sounds like I still do not know.
My dread of it outweighs my curiosity.

But there were a couple of other letters. Rebukes.
One in particular from a Japanese man who indicted
our society, American society, as a whole, asking why
we do not care for our loved ones as they did for us, why
we let someone else pick up the tab. We have broken the
natural cycle of family life, he wrote. People all over the
world attend to their elderly in their own homes, he said,
and it should be an honor to do so.

Oy. Well, why *was* she in a nursing home? Why
wasn't she at home or with her family, where she could
still get mail? Where she could avail herself of promotional discounts, like any American has the right to
do? For one thing, it had gotten to the point where she
needed twenty-four-hour supervision, something none
of us could have provided. As it was, my parents, my
brother, and I had been locked in a fairly tight, near-daily
rotation of visits to my grandmother's apartment for the
past couple of years. In fact, we probably waited longer
than we should have to get her professional help—she
still liked to stand on a chair to change a lightbulb. This

doesn't sound like a big deal until you factor in that the chair was on top of the kitchen table. And another thing: had my grandmother moved in with my parents, we would have had to send my *mother* to a home.

On a cold, grim day in March, with my father at her side, my grandmother dies. We bury her next to my grandfather in a cemetery outside of Philadelphia. There is no formal funeral, only a graveside service presided over by a local rabbi whom none of us know. I do not cry, which is uncharacteristic, because I am an accomplished crier, but I hadn't seen my grandmother in the weeks before her death and I am not one hundred percent sure that she is gone. All that mixing and matching in the nursing home. Perhaps Mrs. Perlmutter, from down the hall, was lying in my grandmother's bed, dressed in her herringbone blazer with the ORT pin on the lapel when she stopped breathing. In my mind, it is likely that I will drive up to the home a few days from now (or a week, or however long I put it off for), and my grandmother will still be there. In fact, during the funeral, I take almost no notice of my grandmother's casket until we are preparing to leave the cemetery. But as I walk away and cast a last, cursory glance back, I am so startled by what I see there that I do a noisy, neck-wrenching double take, like Lou Costello in *Abbot and Costello Meet the Mummy*. Someone has placed a little ivory figurine of a harp seal on top of the coffin. *Her* little ivory figurine of a harp seal. It had lived, along with a Wedgwood ashtray, a University of Pennsylvania shot glass I had given her, and a jade something or other, on the top tier of a three-tiered occasional table in her apartment for as long as I can remember. Its sudden apparitional appearance is utterly spooky, and I grab my mother's arm and point to it. She, too, gasps. Then she remembers that my grandmother had given it to her grandnephew Michael, who was eleven or twelve. He must have decided to return it from whence it came. Clever boy.

They say that the older memories are the ones that endure. That when you can no longer work the telephone or the washing machine, other stuff, stuff that's been in deep storage, is extruded through those gaps and floods the consciousness with ancient goop. A family trip to the seashore in 1908, say. Or the time a horse kicked you in the forehead. I say you, to be inclusive, but I mean my grandfather, specifically, who liked to reference his scar on a regular basis. I had not seen that ivory seal in years, but now I will remember it to my dying day. I will picture the variegated whites of its ivory body, the perfectly rounded curve of its head, and the graceful tilt of its tail. I will remember how, as a child, I loved the hard, smooth feel of it in my hands. I would stroke it tenderly and then I would hold it to my lips and cheek, where it felt cool. It will come back to me at odd moments of my life. It will appear in my dreams and find its way into my stories, like a kick in the head from a horse. And it helps, somehow, to think of my grandmother reunited with it. I hope she will know it when she sees it.

So, why did I want my grandmother to have an American Express card? Why? Why did I want her to have hearing aids and sneakers? Why, for God's sake, did I want her to have Teflon? Was I trying to make her last longer, to keep her sharp, to stave off what was more and more obviously the inevitable? Yes, I was trying to save her, in this sense, but I was also trying to save myself. When my grandmother died, I would no longer be a grandchild. The last little part of my childhood that belonged to me still, because I had a grandparent who was alive, would end, and the prospect of that ending seemed to be something that must be prevented at all costs, even at the risk, however unlikely, of having to return a Garland stove. No matter that I was already a grown-up, or that I worked and had a husband. No matter how badly I'd wanted my *own* child. I still wanted to *be* one. That sounds incredibly selfish but there it is. I am notoriously nostalgic for my childhood and I had counted on my grandmother to be a conduit. The relationship between grandchildren and grandparents is established early and is constructed of some fairly basic elements: playing Scrabble, building houses with playing cards, flipping drink coasters, divvying up small treasures. And who else but a grandmother ever fried bologna? What is remarkable is that these elements do not change with time. They do not age with you, they do not become obsolete. At least they did not for us, per-haps because my grandparents never bought any new games. But that is not why as adults my brother and I often sat on my grandparents' living-room carpet and built card houses. We did it because we still could. And now we can't.

I suppose I wanted my grandmother to have The Card for exactly the reason she did not want it. For its endless possibilities. I felt if she could learn to use an American Express card, she could learn anything, do anything, except go to the Olympics, of course, where Visa still purports to have a stranglehold. It was a test, really, which she failed not only because it was her nature but because she had already begun to suffer from Alzheimer's. She had begun, despite my many protes-tations, her transformation from the grandmother of a child to the grandmother of an adult. And I had begun a transformation of my own.

Leave the Building Quickly

In the house I grew up in we had a ladder made of aluminum tubes connected on each end by metal chains. It was kept loosely folded in a clanky pile at the bottom of the linen closet on the second floor. Should the stairs be blocked in the event of a fire, the ladder could be affixed to the second-story windowsill and draped down the side of the house, allowing us to descend into the rhododendrons below. I don't remember whether we ever had a practice evacuation, but I remember I fantasized endlessly about life-and-death situations during which the ladder would prove indispensable. I also remember that I was anxious about the noise the thing would make clanking against the house as it unfurled.

We had ADT fire and theft protection and something called a panic button, which we were to press in the event of, yes, panic. As with the ladder, I occasionally fantasized about using the panic button, although until I saw the movie *A Clockwork Orange*, I had no specific scenario in mind. After I saw *A Clockwork Orange* I was unable to look at the panic button without feeling panicked. I would like to have a button now to press every time I feel panicked. I wouldn't need anyone to come, I would just enjoy the relief that comes with acknowledging one's feelings.

I've thought about that metal ladder many times, particularly from 1994 to 2003, when I lived in an apartment on the thirty-third floor of a skyscraper. I spent some small part of every day worrying about how I would get down, or even just out, in an emergency. Could I take the stairs to the roof and be plucked off by a rescue worker dangling from a rope lowered by a helicopter? Could I shimmy down a bedsheet to the terrace below ours? Could I really walk down thirty-three flights of stairs with a wet blanket draped over my head? After I had my first child, I imagined myself standing on our tiny terrace, screaming to the helicopter pilot that was hovering a few feet away, "Take my baby! Take my baby!" as Marg Helgenberger, the prostitute-turned-mother did, in one of the final episodes of *China Beach*. Long before the Twin Towers came down, I envisioned airplanes crashing right through our west-facing windows. Sometimes the roar of passing jets was so loud that I just stood at the window and watched them miss us, seemingly by a few feet. I hated that apartment.

My fear of fire began, as so many things did, in Florida in the '70s. We were visiting my grandparents' apartment in the Ocean-South building of the Hemispheres, a renowned four-building complex in Hallandale, and on the evening news one night was a segment on the flammability of children's sleepwear, which was surprising, because up until that evening I was under the impression that only one show—*Perry Mason*—was broadcast over the South Florida airwaves. As I remember it, the news anchor was reporting a lawsuit against a pajama manufacturer, brought by the family of a child who'd been horribly burned when, somehow or other, his pajamas went up in flames. They gave a demonstration of how quickly the pajamas, once ignited, became a pajama flambé, although no one explained how the pajamas in question had, in fact, caught fire. So, I deduced that flammable pajamas spontaneously combusted. I woke up screaming that night and for many nights after. My mother comforted me again and again, and, in time, the trauma acquired the benign soft focus of a distant dream. As I matured, my thoughts turned elsewhere, like to the story my mother told about her good friend's nephew, who was burned at a high school party by an overturned tiki light, or to the driver's ed classic *Cars That Crash and Burn*.

Do you know why a race-car driver wears epaulets despite the fact that epaulets would seem in every manner contrary to the aesthetic of a race-car driver?

It is so that in the event of a crash he may be pulled from the flaming wreckage of his car.

The summer before our son, John, began nursery school, I answered a questionnaire intended to help his teachers know what kind of child he is. I wrote that he was a bright, chatty, joyful child, inquisitive and funny, and oh, you know, basically perfect. A perfect specimen of the small-child race. I gave him a real A-plus profile, managing only to avoid extolling his astonishing physical beauty. But at the end of the questionnaire, when asked if there was anything special they should know about my child, I broke down and admitted what I believed to be his only weakness: he was afraid of sudden loud noises.

Sometime in the second month of school, after the children had successfully completed the break-in process—a lengthy period during which the parents sit outside the classroom reading the paper so their kids don't feel abandoned—the school performed its first fire drill of the year, neglecting to warn its youngest students in advance. An oversight, but, I think, in retrospect, all would agree a costly one.

The kid was traumatized. There's no other way to put it. He cried and shook and was completely freaked out, particularly by the flashing light on the wall. (For the nonexistent deaf students, I imagine.) He set off a chain reaction of crying, shaking children, all of whom were told in gently perky tones that they were just "practicing leaving the building quickly, that's all," as if they were just practicing going down the slide or smiling or touching their noses with their index fingers. Then this quivering puddle was lined up single-file in the hallway, led down five flights of stairs, and finally poured out onto the sidewalk.

Practicing leaving the building quickly. That's a good one. It sounded familiar though. I'd heard it before, or something like it. Then I remembered. I was in Harry's Shoes and I'd seen a little girl place several single shoes, chosen from the display racks, on a chair in front of her grandmother. The girl held up one with a little heel. The grandmother shook her head and said, "What if you have to leave the building quickly?"

The day after the fire alarm, John would not enter his classroom. It was all I could do to get him in the building. The incredible ease and grace with which he had separated from me—it took him about five minutes—and adjusted to the routine of school was replaced by the most profound dread. He stood quaking at the door to Room 10 and could not be coaxed inside. Any suggestion that he cross the threshold sent him hopping away, dancing around the hallway like a boxer (welterweight) at his debut prizefight, one step forward and then three back, in horrible anticipation of the whomp of that first punch in the face. Sure, it was coming; what in the world could he do about it? Get the hell out of there? Maybe.

Each day for weeks it went like this. His teacher, Adrienne, would come to the door and crouch down.

"Hi John."

"Oh, uh, hi Adrienne."

"Do you want to come in? We're making Play-Doh today, and we have the blocks you like out and ..."

"No thanks Adrienne, I'm just going to stay out here in the hall for a while with my mom. You go ahead with the Play-Doh, that's okay, and I'll just be here."

He wouldn't say anything about the alarm, but every few minutes he would crane his neck around the doorway to look up at the clear box that housed the fire alarm's flashing light.

"Is it flashing, Mom?" he'd ask.

"No, it isn't flashing and I promise it won't flash today."

Each day his best friend, Sam, would come to the door.

"John!"

John and Sam met when they were three months old. Even though they saw each other every day they behaved like brothers separated during the war and then miraculously reunited upon release from their respective P.O.W. camps. Sam! John! Sam! John! There were hugs and slaps on the back. It was a beautiful thing.

"Oh, hi Sam." It was so uncharacteristic of John to

be subdued when confronted with Sam that a chill went through me.

"John, come in."

"I'm sorry, Sam. I can't."

Each day, after about ten or fifteen minutes, I was able to sort of trick him into joining the class. I would bring out a toy and then, after he played with it for a few minutes, tell him he needed to put it back in its place. After a couple of rounds of "You do it"/"No, you do it," he would wade in.

We spoke of the fire alarm daily for the rest of the school year. And the year after that. At some point each afternoon and often again in the evening, John would ask me to tell him the story of the loud noise. Over time, it acquired the tone of a fairy tale. I would begin with "Once upon a time" and then incorporate all of John's activities that day up until the moment of the alarm, the names of the kids in his class, what they'd had for snack, which activity was interrupted. Sometimes I would sit on our green couch and David would sit in the big red chair, with John perched somewhere between us, and we would take turns telling slightly varied versions of the story, over and over, a sort of cleansing ritual I imagine might take place at a Native American tribal celebration. First the chief tells a powerful story of a young brave in peril, then someone else chants or sings the same story while a bunch of men and women, with the story painted on their limbs and torsos, get up to dance/mime it. No matter how the story is told, the ending is always the same. The young brave triumphs. He has come face-to-face with his worst fear, possibly an Apache or maybe a wild boar, and he has prevailed. This was what John was waiting to hear. This was why we told the story. He needed to be reminded that he would prevail. To this day I regret not writing a song for John called "Fire Alarm: No Problem," and playing it on my guitar. I still might.

I thought John's fear of alarms might affect his love of firemen and fire trucks, but it did not, and I soon realized that Fire Alarm was the name of a sound, not the harbinger of an event. So, our household declared a moratorium on sudden loud noises. All phone ringers save one were turned off. The doorbell of our new apartment, which did not work when we moved in, was encouraged to continue so. The buzzer on the phone that connects us to the doormen downstairs was turned to its lowest volume, so low that often we didn't heed its call and the Chinese food delivery guy was turned away from the building.

The truth is that I do not like sudden loud noises either. When the telephone rings after midnight, I go into full flail. *Someone is dead! Someone is dead!* I disappear beneath the blankets and fold my arms over my head as though we are in the midst of an air-raid drill.

I like to think that the kind of compulsive fear to which I am susceptible is not something you instill in your children on purpose. You do it by accident, by being overprotective, jumpy, and singing them songs at bedtime about doomed farm animals. There's one song I've been singing since I was a child and now I sing it to John. I don't know what the name of it is but the refrain goes, "Dona Dona Dona." I have no idea what "Dona Dona Dona" means except that by the end of the song, a little calf is on his way to becoming a veal chop, after having been lectured by the farmer that it is the calf's own fault, for not being a bird. But it has a lovely tune!

Then there's my rendition of the Muffin Man song. I've never known the correct words to this, but some time ago there was a television movie about a pedophile, called *Do You Know the Muffin Man?*, and I think, subconsciously, this informed my own version: "Do you know the muffin man, the muffin man, the muffin man? Do you know the muffin man? Stay away from him!" This is not dissimilar in subtext from my "Pop Goes the Weasel": "All around the mulberry bush, the monkey chased the weasel. The monkey did something he should not have done. Pop, goes the weasel." What the heck's that all about? Why would I sing that? Well, it has the right number of syllables, and so fits into the song's meter. Musicality is important. But also, isn't there something suspicious about the monkey chasing the weasel, and then, pop? What is pop? Does the weasel just explode? Does it get an erection? What? What? It doesn't matter what the exact words are. There is chasing and then popping. It's grotesque. Somebody tell me what it means.

Despite all of this, I have done my best to shield John from my pathology. I have instead foisted its weight upon David, and aside from the annoyance, he isn't any worse for the wear. I truly believe John's condition is genetic. I didn't bring up a tenderhearted, slightly panicky child: I produced one at birth. Meaning, I don't think it's my fault and yet it still is.

In every room in every building John enters, he stops to look for the fire alarm system. In every apartment, every restaurant, every school, he will stand in the doorway and inquire of anyone within earshot as to the possibility of a fire alarm drill. He will on occasion balk and refuse to enter a space. I don't know what his judgment is based upon—instinct, a precocious understanding of the laws of probability, low blood sugar. I have learned to try not to bully him in, to trust him and honor his fear. After all, I'm as wary as he is. Come to think of it, having John around is a little like having my own canary in a coal mine. I should always send him on ahead, let him suss things out, weigh the risks, locate the exits. Then, when he gives the all-clear, I'll follow. In flats, of course.

Kaplan's Sister

You know how they say about certain people, "His door was always open"? Well, my brother's door was always closed. When we were growing up, I never just walked into his room and plopped onto his bed. The few times I tried it, he regarded me coolly and said, "Yes?" I was not permitted to touch his stuff, even if I was looking for something that might belong to me. I once used his ChapStick and was persona even more non grata for six months after. On rare occasions, I was invited in for music education. My brother introduced me to Elvis Costello, Bruce Springsteen, Queen, Supertramp, Squeeze, Joe Jackson. Try as I might, I could not interest him in John Denver or Bread. Once a year, we convened in his room with the lights off and listened to Orson Welles's radio version of *The War of the Worlds*.

When I was thirteen and he was fifteen, he let me

read his *National Lampoon* magazines, although I was not allowed to discuss them with him. This would have been helpful, as there definitely were things I did not understand, like the story about the guy who woke up one morning with breasts and a vagina and was promptly molested by his friends.

In fact, I don't know that I remember a single discussion between us from those days. What did we talk about? I read other people's memoirs and I can't understand how they recall so much. Endless conversations are recounted word for word, childhood scenes painted in minute detail, who walked in when, who wore a brown hat, who ate the last doughnut. How do they do it? Hypnosis? Sometimes the images from my childhood are so vague, so diaphanous as to effectively erase them. I remember I have a brother. Isn't that enough?

I asked my brother about this recently. I said, "I don't remember what we talked about." He said, "I didn't talk to you." He admits now that as an older brother, he was simply not capable of viewing me as a person. I was an extension of my parents, who were, to his mind, intrusive and controlling. The funny thing is that my brother's activities didn't require parental oversight. He didn't have anything in particular to hide. He didn't drink or do drugs or beat kids up. The reason he appeared hungover on school mornings was because he stayed up late most nights watching Johnny Carson on an old TV in his room. When our parents went out on a Saturday night, we brought *The Peanuts Treasury* and *Peanuts Classics* to the dinner table and silently passed the Cap'n Crunch and the milk until both were empty. After that, one of us would watch TV in the den and one would go upstairs to watch our parents' TV in their bedroom.

I remember one night, in a rare collaborative effort, we built a Lincoln Logs science research center and shot a Super-8 movie, using rubber monsters to portray the terrifying result of a scientific experiment gone awry. We tied thread to their legs and pulled them out through the Lincoln Logs walls, which then crashed down around them. They evaded capture by a company of G.I. Joes, to a soundtrack featuring Sweet's *Little Willy*, which we played on a tape recorder while the movie ran.

I like to date my grown-up relationship with my brother to his acquisition of our grandparents' gigantic 1965 light blue Oldsmobile. Somewhere around the time my grandfather turned eighty and my brother sixteen, my father decided that my grandfather should stop driving so that my brother, newly licensed, could start. This convenient arrangement was not as callous as it appeared. My grandfather, while robust for his age, had nevertheless survived a heart attack, and various other ailments plagued him, including cataracts, which are not particularly driver-friendly. The blue Oldsmobile appeared one Saturday in the driveway of our house in Connecticut, and on Sunday my grandparents went home to Manhattan on the train.

They don't make cars like the Olds anymore. It had a matching light blue interior with silvery blue vinyl bench seats. It had a blue and silver dash and a hard, skinny, blue steering wheel. To adjust for the height of the driver, the entire front bench had to be lurched forward or back, with everyone helping. The light blue hood of the Olds was so long and seemed so far away that it created its own sort of traveling-horizon effect. Seated by the passenger-side window, I was literally several feet from my brother, which supported his perception that I was not there at all. Nevertheless, in those early days, beneath the chug of the engine ran a hum of mutual excitement; the portion of our lives during which we were at the sole mercy of adults was nearing its end. Freedom was upon us!

Soon my brother was permitted to drive to school in the mornings, me along with him. He occasionally gave me a ride to a friend's house, picked me up from play rehearsal or basketball practice, and took me with him into town to shop for records in the back room at Klein's. Occasionally—that is, when it could not be avoided— my brother brought me along to his friends' houses, almost as though he'd just happened to have someone with him, like the dog. I was allowed to come in primarily because he knew he shouldn't leave me in the car in the heat. I sat silently during these forays, equally bored and titillated. I was hoping for the chance to see what he and his friends did besides play and replay the recently released *This Year's Model* and assemble ham radios from Heathkits. They were junior scientists and technophiles, who every spring ran the lights and sound for the school musical and spent many weekend nights watching the movie *Gumball Rally* or driving around town pretending to be in it. They peppered their conversation with made-up words like "motton," which meant "a little bit," as in, "I'll have just a motton of juice, thanks" or "I'll be ready in a motton." Motton was derived from the name Tad Martin, a famous character on a popular soap opera that none of them watched. A "tad" of something is a little bit of something. Motton was just Martin with a British accent.

The term for me in this lexicon was "Kaplan's Sister." My husband tells me that when his older sister's friends passed him in the hall at school and yelled out "Hey, Little Froels," he felt fantastic. Somehow Kaplan's Sister did not quite have that effect on me, because, I think, my brother's disinterest rubbed off on his friends. I was less Kaplan's Sister than maybe Kaplan's Phantom Limb, or Kaplan's Teratoma, a thing with hair and teeth and other human stuff, which he carried around but which required little or no attention. I remember going with my brother's gang to see *Monty Python and the Holy Grail.* We laughed and laughed. We literally fell out of our seats. For months after, those guys went all over town saying NI! to each other. I said NI! a couple of times but no one responded. It was sad. NI! NI!—and then nothing.

One dark night, in that first winter of my brother's driving career, we hit a patch of ice on a curving country road and spun around and around. We finally came to a stop in the opposite lane, facing back the way we came, miraculously managing not to hit anything or have anything hit us. My brother said "Whoa" and "Shit." He took a deep breath and straightened out the car. We drove around the curve and down a hill to a stop sign. Then he turned to me and said, "I don't think we should mention this to Mom and Dad." "Okay," I said. A charge went through me. We had a secret! There would be others, of course. We were a united front. And this was only the beginning. Next we would organize a weekly co-ed touch football game.

Or not. When I was fifteen, my brother took me out to Sherwood Island State Park and let me drive the Oldsmobile around the parking lot and up and down the short road that ran along the beach. The plan was that I would be so skilled a driver that after I got my license at sixteen, it would not be necessary for him to chaperone me.

Our father, who'd been pining for a convertible and was perhaps, in a fashion, similarly celebrating his emancipation from his children, bought a Fiat Spider, not the most family-oriented car. It replaced our mother's twelve-year-old Mercedes lemon. Well, not quite. She did not get the Spider, but rather our father's horrific diesel Cadillac, which went from zero to sixty in fifteen minutes. My brother and I have just a few precious memories of riding alone in the Spider with the music blaring and my long hair slapping our faces. It had become clear that the engine of the Oldsmobile was about to drop through the bottom of the car, and the day our father declared it condemned he let my brother drive the Spider to school. That was the last time I saw it. At lunchtime, as my brother was pulling out of a space in the school lot, it was struck a fatal blow by one of two drag-racing Camaros.

We both rode the bus for a while after that, but then my sixteenth birthday arrived and our father bought a flesh-colored Saab hatchback off the showroom floor, having read that it was one of the safest cars on the road. There was a tape deck in the car and my brother spent hours in his room putting his entire record collection onto Maxell tapes. My brother taught me to play car tag, where you must continually try to pass a friend's car without speeding or doing anything blatantly illegal. He stopped playing this after a policeman called my parents one night at eleven o'clock and asked them if they owned a white Saab, at which point they presumed the worst. I stopped playing the day my friend Mary Beth rear-ended a couple in a rental car, who were in town because their son was hospitalized after having fallen through a skylight, probably while playing some equally stupid game.

Eventually my brother and I found ourselves going to the same parties. Some of my friends started dating some of his friends, although I still didn't know if he himself had a girlfriend. I didn't know what he thought about sex or school or politics or anything that wasn't music. Frankly, I was waiting for him to tell me what he thought; how else would I figure out what *I* thought? Unfortunately, more than anything else, my brother valued independence. Or maybe *privacy* is the right word. Privacy of the mind, of the body, of the will. When he was around eight or nine, he miscalculated the difference between the date of our parents' wedding and that of his own birth, and remained secretly convinced for several years that he was a bastard. Perhaps this precipitated some kind of familial break from which he never recovered. But, as I said, he was not the typical rebel. Rather he was a resistance fighter, executing small acts of self-determination, hiding out in safe houses of his own making, i.e., his room, the car, the shower, and God only knew where else.

He was also annoying. If you asked him to do something, say, the dishes, or for help with homework, his answer would be yes, but only on the condition that the thing would be done his way, when he was good and ready. Our mother was a timely sort of woman, and

there was often a discrepancy between Sandra Time and
Steve Time. For example, after dinner, it was my brother's job to take the garbage out. He knew it was his job,
and he planned to do the job, but *when* he did it, well,
that was up to him. If our mother nagged him about it,
as she invariably would, he'd accuse her of not trusting
him. My brother did not like to do something because he
was asked. It was as though he needed time to *forget* he'd
been asked, so it would seem to him that he was doing it
of his own accord. Maybe that is what Steve Time was
for—the transit of power.

"He was the most delightful child. You both were,"
says our mother. Implied is the corollary, "What happened?"

My brother went off to college and I have almost no
memory of him from those years, except for this: I visited him once, during his freshman year, and we had
a conversation in his room about a girl he liked and I
think he may have let me tell him something personal
as well and then he took me to a party. I spent the rest
of the weekend elated that we had made a connection.
Ever hopeful, I presumed once again, and once again
incorrectly, that this was the dawn of a new era.

I ended up at the same college, but really, there was
almost no way for me to know he was there, too. We
ran into each other sporadically and he seemed happy

enough to see me and introduce me around. "This is my sister," he'd say. He came to see me in plays, and one year, after he brought some friends to see a play in which I appeared on stage in a black lace teddy, the moniker Kaplan's Sister acquired a slight luster. I developed a nice relationship with my brother's girlfriend, who, when I first arrived at school, showed up without my brother but with a hammer to see if she could help me hang pictures. They were now living together off campus in a small basement apartment. The first time I visited, I was struck by the unmade bed in the tiny bedroom. It wasn't the fact that it was unmade, although, coming from our mother's home, that could have been the issue, but rather it occurred to me for the first time that my brother must be having sex. Of course he was, of *course*. I looked at my brother. Did he look different? Different from what? I didn't know where to store this information. It was as though I had come upon our dog, Catcher, playing Mille Bornes with his dog friends. Thankfully, there, in the corner of the bedroom, was something familiar—a gigantic Velveeta box his friends had perhaps stolen from a store display and given him as a joke because he still ate Velveeta, a rubbery, cheese-like substance that seems intended only for consumption by small children.

Most of our "quality time" was spent driving back and forth between school and home for holidays and vacations. Once, while traveling to New York City to meet our parents for dinner, I asked my brother what he and his girlfriend were doing about birth control. I started to tell him that I had lost my virginity, and he stopped me, gently. He didn't need to know what I was doing, he said. But I was bursting with my news, so as soon as we arrived at the restaurant in New York, I had no choice but to tell my mother.

We drove home from school together for the last time that summer, in good spirits, blasting old ELO or Talking Heads. I sat, as I often did, with my legs up on the dash, bare feet against the windshield. As we sped by the Molly Pitcher rest stop, I stretched my arms and flexed my feet and suddenly there was a loud noise, as though something hard had hit the windshield, and a huge crack appeared down the center of it. Once again my brother uttered the words "Whoa" and "Shit." He thought a rock had hit us but I knew immediately that I somehow had put pressure on a weak spot in the glass and cracked it. I told my brother this and he said, as he had long ago, "Let's not mention that to Mom and Dad." We went with the rock story.

We ended this chapter as we began, in the car, with a small secret. It wasn't much but I took it. Not long after that, my brother got a job and a car and moved away.

There is a show on public television, called *Joy of Painting*. It is in reruns now, because its longtime host, Bob

Ross, has died. If you have never seen *Joy of Painting*, it consists entirely of Bob Ross, a crunchy granola–looking white guy with a reddish-brown afro, standing at an easel, demonstrating the art of oil painting. The paintings themselves are ultra-realistic landscapes depicting setting suns or mountain streams or snow-peaked fir trees. Each painting has a name like "Sunrise over the Bay" or "Autumn Homecoming" or some such, and they most resemble the paintings that are advertised every so often on television as being for sale on Memorial Day or Presidents' Day weekends at a blowout at Shea Stadium or at one of several Long Island Marriott Hotels. I don't actively seek out *Joy of Painting*, because that would be insane, but every time I come upon it I find myself unable to turn away. I become transfixed and watch for whatever time remains in the hour.

There are a couple of reasons, the first being that each show was dedicated to completing an entire work of art, start to finish, and watching Bob Ross execute this feat was like watching a time-lapse movie of a caterpillar turning into a butterfly. With just a flick of his #2 fan brush or a deft turn of his painting knife, abstract blobs turned into cumulous clouds, a row of lines turned into a forest, shadows emerged to render two dimensions into three. It was magic. You wouldn't hang it in your garage but it was magic nonetheless.

The second reason it was impossible to switch the channel was Bob himself. In his gentle, folksy voice, he guided you through the execution of the painting step-by-step, tool-by-tool, color-by-color. He presumed you were out there in TV land, with your canvas and your easel, your palette of Van Dyke Brown and Indian Red and Cadmium Yellow, ready to paint along with him. He never scolded; he was neither pedantic nor patronizing. He showed you the way, all the while encouraging your individuality. Maybe you wanted the reflection of the sun on the lake just so, but it was okay if you didn't. It was *your* painting, your world. Whatever you decided, Bob was there for you.

And, if you needed more time, you could order his video in the mail.

I could have used someone like Bob Ross, someone to show me how things worked, someone to tell me how much Titanium White to mix into the Pthalo Blue for the mountain stream or where to lay in the Dark Sienna slashes so they look like branches jutting out along the shoreline. Perhaps Bob was so popular, so beloved, because a blank canvas is just too daunting.

In fact, there should have been a show called *Joy of Adolescence*. We all want someone who is not our mother to reassure us that we are doing fine. Well, this was not a role that interested my brother. And I see now that he could not have taught me what I wanted to know. My brother and I had different pictures of what our youth looked like. I wanted something Bob Ross might have painted, something obvious, titled maybe "Romance

Under the Bleachers with the Captain of the Football Team." My brother seemed content to paint an inscrutable Dadaist dreamscape, the interpretation of which he owed no one, not even me. Since my brother didn't seem interested in anyone's approval, I'm sure he couldn't imagine why I would want his. I did, though. I thought he was smart and funny and I wanted him to think that I was, too. Here's something else: he was, to put it simply, male. I didn't have a lot of attention from the opposite sex in those days and I don't think it would be Freudian/icky to say that my brother's counted. His approval of me would have given me confidence, and it would have set an example for others, conferred status, implied I was worthy of their notice. In truth, I suppose, I was not so much dreaming of other brotherdom as other *Cindy*dom. Any time my brother took me into his confidence — or better, into his world — I felt the state of Cindydom was elevated, however briefly, to a new plateau.

Looking back, I'm not sure my brother had any status of his own, much less some to confer upon me. Whether he did or not, I'm pretty sure it did not concern him much. He felt fine as he was. I might have learned something from that.

Eventually, being Kaplan's Sister bore its sweeter fruit. In his mid-twenties my brother bought a small sailboat, which we often sailed together off City Island. He was then dating his future wife, and we talked about her, just a little, and about his work, just a little. Sometimes we made fun of our parents, and sometimes we just sailed. I helped him pick a couch for his apartment, and then, later, a diamond ring. He and his best friend took me to see Elvis Costello at the Beacon Theater. I went with him and his wife on vacation to Nantucket as sort of a guest/au pair after their first daughter was born. Last summer, David and the kids and I spent a week with his family in a farmhouse in Provence. I don't know that we spoke any more in France than we ever do, but may I say the proximity was profoundly enjoyable. There was, of course, the year or two in there when he didn't call me at all, and didn't realize he didn't, but what are you going to do?

And, happily, it has turned out that my brother is a devoted father and husband, and I am relieved to report that it doesn't seem as though anyone refers to his family as Kaplan's Wife and Kaplan's Daughters. He is a considerate and loving son; presumably the bastard issue has worked itself out. And he's a good brother. I count on him and he allows that. He is always there when I need him, or perhaps to put it another way, he's now as much brother as I need. Or perhaps again, contrary to everything I have written here, he has, in fact, trained me well.

Sis Boom Bah

When I arrived at sleepaway camp at the age of nine, I was so small and spindly that I was unable to serve the ball in Newcomb. In case you don't know what it is, Newcomb is a game played with a volleyball on a volleyball court by children too young and weak to return the ball with their fists or open palms. The ball is simply thrown from one side of the court and is caught on the other. The first side to drop the ball or throw it into the net during one of these volleys loses the point.

Who was this man Newcomb? An Englishman, I imagine, concave-chested and pale, haunted by the memory of getting towel-whipped in the shower by the Eton rugby team.

As I say, I was not strong enough to throw the ball over the net from the base line, even though I had two chances, like in tennis. Following each failed attempt, my team, the Yellow Team, would sing out, "That's all right, that's okay, we still love you anyway." It's the universal song of unconditional support. And it sounds pretty friendly until you parse it. "We still love you *anyway.*" If the song stopped at "you," there'd be no problem, but that "anyway"—it really sticks in the craw. *Anyway.* I was small but I wasn't stupid. "Anyway" is a qualifier, meaning, in this case, "even though." Even though you stink. Even though you are a liability to us. Even though we might lose to the Green Team because of you. We still love you even though we hate you.

Over the course of that first summer, I noticed that girls who were actually *good* at things never had to hear that song. Girls who could throw the ball over the net or into the basket, girls who could water-ski without falling thirty times while everyone is waiting for a turn, girls who made spectacular lanyards—they had another song. It started with "Sis Boom Bah" and ended with "Ra!"

My parents, or what I can remember of them from that period—my father wore sideburns and my mother had espadrilles in a variety of summery colors—were optimistic about my chances for success in the world. My father ran a thriving computer business. My mother, a housewife, had gone to the very elite Bennington College and regularly read impenetrable, eight-hundred-page historical biographies in her spare time, for fun.

Her gifts, however, were not confined to an encyclo-
pedic knowledge of dead monarchs. She did lovely
crewel work and after only a year in the suburbs she
was awarded the Most Improved Player trophy by the
Westport Women's Bowling League. My brother, Steve,
was a smarty-pants (I was a smart-*ass*, which is not the
same thing) with an early understanding of mathemat-
ical formulae. Whenever I came to him for help with
my math homework, he patently refused to guide me
through a difficult problem or two unless I was willing
to sit through a two-hour-long symposium on the cor-
responding theorem. If we'd had an overhead projector
he'd have used it.

Clearly, these were not people to whom patronizing
jingles were sung. These were Sis Boom Bah people and
it was entirely possible that they expected I would be
one as well. How disappointed would they be when they
found out I was not? Enough to sing about it? I came to
the conclusion that there was really only one way to be
sure my parents couldn't claim to "love me" in spite of
my failings, and that was to have none. But just in case
I did, I also decided it might be best if I did not allow
my parents to see me *do* anything, in the event that they
would drive away afterward, shaking their heads and
warbling, "That's alright, that's okay, we still love her
anyway."

I used to study ballet, and every year there was a re-
cital in which we performed a dance based on the legend

of Stonehenge. For this dance the corps de ballet was divided into three sections: stones, Druids, and ghosts. The best dancers got to be ghosts, who swooped and flitted around wearing layers of lovely, gossamer scarves over their heads and arms. The middling group were Druids, and they strode somberly in hooded cloaks, hands clasped piously before them. Finally came the stones, shrouded in gray, who stood stock-still in a circle the entire dance. By my third year of ballet, I had achieved the exalted status of ghost, although I did not inform my family of this. The pressure was too much for me. Better to let them think of me as an excellent stone.

Over time, I became what I now smirkingly refer to as a "well-rounded person." I was reasonably good at everything. I was an A-minus student, I could sing and dance, and I played a variety of sports. I starred in educational filmstrips about suicidal pregnant girls and teens on drugs and I painted landscapes in watercolor. This was how I got into college—on the "well-rounded" platform. I did everything but spin plates on sticks and eat fire. I couldn't help myself. I was still operating under the delusion that success equals love. The more things I was good at, the more people would love me. My one saving grace was that I was too shy to become an actual ass-kisser.

It was stressful to be so competent all the time and I started to resent the effort, nursing the surly belief that others did not fully recognize my true worth. Well, who knew what my true worth was? I sure as hell didn't. Well-rounded people tend to be sort of invisible, nothing in particular makes us stand out. To this day I harbor a pathological envy of child prodigies — Tracy Austin, Michael Jackson, Buffy from *Family Affair*. It doesn't matter how fucked up they are or even if they are dead, as long as they'd been truly great at just one thing.

No one was more surprised than my parents when I went into a graduate acting program after college. It seemed counterintuitive. I did not *appear* to be an actor type of person. I never stood on the kitchen table belting out "Tomorrow." I was, however, particularly fond of singing Aldonza's song from *Man of La Mancha*: "I was born on a dung heap to die on a dung heap, a strumpet men use and forget!" I did not have that bohemian look frequently mistaken for a sign of inner artistry — almost but not quite frizzy hair (some jerk called it "ethereal" once) and a high, pinched voice, like a little girl's but louder — the kind of voice that says I'm an *actress*, I'm *acting*! I was painfully aware of these shortcomings and thought that any suggestion from me that I was "actor material" would be met with disbelief if not ridicule by my peers and teachers. I also decided not to mention it to my parents in case they felt the need to unconditionally support me.

I loved acting school. I believed that I was, for the first time in my life, doing the exact thing I should be doing. Of course, I spent way too much time perfecting the breathing exercises and trying to figure out how to make a blue enamel bracelet look like Queen Elizabeth's crown for a scene from *Richard III*, neither of which activity got me particularly noticed. The actors who were the least reliable, the most temperamental, and did the most hurling, which is what we called getting up to do a scene without having any idea what you were doing, got the most attention. Something about their unpredictability gave teachers and directors the idea that they were exciting actors. The less disciplined they were, the more talent it was presumed they had. This drove me crazy, because I rarely, if ever, hurled, and I thought most of those actors were full of shit. Nevertheless, once again, it was clear to me that my merit-based approach was paradoxically leading me away from, rather than toward, success.

Like every other actor in the known world, I also worked as a waitress. Waitressing paid for acting jobs which did not pay for themselves. Actors say they do it because it is flexible, but the truth, I realized after a while, is that it is something else as well. It is a performance opportunity. Every night you memorize the specials, like a little food monologue, which you then perform, with feeling, for paying guests. You get to perform your monologue many times a night, varying your emphasis, trying different readings, say, stressing the pork loin at one table and the hangar steak at another, speaking, if you dare, with a foreign accent or a brogue or a lisp.

Waiters came and went with alarming frequency. A few were called away to understudy Billy Bigelow in a bus-and-truck production of *Carousel* or play Caliban in a version of *The Tempest* set, as all off-off-Broadway productions of Shakespeare are, in Nazi Germany. And many waiters were hired and then fired by management in the space of a few days for one of two reasons: total incompetence or "just because." But after I'd been at one restaurant for a few months, I began to notice a disturbing trend—disturbing, that is, to me. Waiters blew off shifts all the time. Perhaps, after a night of doing ecstasy, someone just sort of forgot he had a job. Or someone needed a personal day or more sleep or a haircut. Or maybe someone had slapped the owner during a late-night catfight about a cold decaf cappuccino. Yet they all turned up again a shift or two later and got their jobs back while remaining resolutely unapologetic. I wasn't sure if these people were brave or just stupid. And I realized I didn't care. I was too busy admiring their thoughtlessness, their flouting of authority. True to form, I never lashed out at management or patrons, no matter how often they were down on their knees, begging for a lashing. I never left food to congeal under the heat lamp in the kitchen or let a salad go limp. I never called in sick. I was not independent enough to get myself fired. I never even inspired a reprimand or a talking-to. I was neither devil-may-care nor even will-fully lackadaisical. As waiters came and went, I began to see getting fired as less a humiliation than a badge of honor. Unfortunately, I was still too much of a goody-two-shoes to permit the first or deserve the second.

But then something strange and amazing happened. After several months at the restaurant, I started to feel like I was part of a team. But this was a different kind of team than the Yellow Team. This was a team who, were they to sing "That's all right, that's okay, we still love you anyway" when I broke a cork into a $80 bottle of wine, besides sounding fantastic, like the New York Gay Men's Choir, would actually mean it. This team, the Waiter Team, had an entirely different set of standards. Being the best, most conscientious waiters they could be was not necessarily one of them. It was more important to be fit and trim, be amusing to be around, and/or able to recite verbatim climactic scenes from the Susan Hayward film *I Want to Live!* Sure, they were good waiters, but mostly because good waiters *look* better than bad waiters. Competence is just more flattering.

The latest brain research suggests that people develop different talents at different times. That's just how the brain works. For example, some children learn to read at four, some at eight. So, at this late date, decades after my peers, and with the support of the Waiter Team, I developed, for lack of a better word, or perhaps there is no better word, *attitude*. It wasn't something grumpy or obvious; I didn't start saying "harrumph" a lot or snap my fingers in a large arc, as I had often seen expertly done. Rather, it was subtle—a thing which expressed itself with a deviousness that made reprisal almost impossible. When a diner said or did something I didn't like, I gave him a look. A fleeting, restrained look, slipped into the moment after one blink and before the next. It was a look that in translation fell somewhere between "Has the world stopped spinning on its axis?" and "I hear a dog barking in the distance."

At first I employed The Look judiciously, restricting its use to the restaurant and the occasional play rehearsal—some actors really asked for it—but it eventually took on a life of its own. I'm sure under extreme conditions I achieved a kind of terrifying, eye-popping Marty Feldman effect. Who could blame me? People were such jerks. Why shouldn't I be one, too? It felt good to be a jerk. It felt both liberating and empowering, like I was F.D.R. after he had decided to stop appeasing Germany.

I left waitressing of my own accord (how else?) in order to have more time for auditions and low-paying acting jobs. I had also begun to book commercials, which paid well and, happily, did not require me to wear khakis and a man's tie and ask people I had known in college if they'd like another plate of crab fritters. My latest was a commercial for an H.M.O., in which I was supposed to play the nurse in a patient's nightmare medical scenario, as if there is any other kind. I was to be paid time and a half in order to fly around on cables wearing a crisp white dress and a peaked cap.

Sometime in the week before every commercial shoot, there is a fitting, during which you are measured and appraised and decisions are made about your clothing and general appearance. I don't usually get cast for my general appearance; I get cast for my ability to *be* odd without *looking* odd. At the fitting for the H.M.O. spot, I was given the once-over, my measurements were taken, and I was sent on my way. Or so I had thought. While I was waiting by the elevator, a woman I did not know approached me. I later found out she was the producer.

"Hi, just a second."

"Hi."

"Hi, listen, can anything be done with your hair?"

Now, my hair has been an issue my whole life. It never looks brushed. It is wavy in an irregular way and I am not remotely interested in blow-drying it into some kind of recognizable style. That I have neither the desire nor the patience to discuss this with others is no one's fault but my mother's. Anyway, the woman clearly did not intend her question to be rhetorical.

"What do you have in mind?" I asked—politely, I thought.

"I mean, is this how it always looks?"

"No." So I lied, so what.

"It's just hanging there. Could it look more polished, maybe bigger?"

"I'm sure it could. It could do whatever you want it to do."

Why can't these people remember that there will be professional hair and makeup people on set the day of the shoot? They're at *every* shoot. If they wanted, they could make me look like Ava Gardner. They could make Keith Richards look like Ava Gardner.

"Hmm." She examined me. "Maybe you could wear a wig."

"A wig?"

That is what my mouth said: "A wig?" My eyes said: Hark, I hear an Irish wolfhound in the distance.

"Yes. A wig would be much, much better."

My mouth: "Honestly, you can do anything with my hair. It is very agreeable hair."

My eyes: Harumph, harumph, snap!

"I'm not sure. It looks flat. I'm not sure we can fix that. Let's get you a wig, okay? What are you doing this afternoon? There's a wig store on Fourteenth Street. We'll have someone meet you there."

Mouth: "I have a doctor's appointment at one. Anytime after that is fine."

Eyes: *I was born on a dung heap to die on a dung heap, a strumpet men use and forget!*

Later my agent called.

"Cindy, I'm so sorry, but you've been released."

"What?" I said.

"The producer called. She thought you had a bad attitude."

"That's not true," I said. "She didn't like my hair. I couldn't have been more accommodating. Have you ever known me to give attitude?" A reputation as a good girl isn't always such a terrible thing.

"I know. I know you don't give attitude. I'm sorry. They probably decided they want someone else and are saying that so they can try to get out of paying you for the shoot. But they won't. Don't worry. And I think you have very nice hair."

I pretended to myself to be perplexed for a few minutes. How could this have happened? But I knew. I knew exactly how it had happened. I'd given that woman The Look. *But good,* as my grandmother would say. The more I thought about it, the better I felt. And it wasn't about the wig. I'd wear a wig. For time and a half I'd wear a basket of fruit on my head. But I wasn't going to be insulted. I'd waited all my life to stop taking people's shit lying down. If I was going to take it at all, I would take it standing up, like a waiter. Maybe one day, with luck and hard work, I'd get myself fired for incompetence, too.

I don't mean to suggest that a bad attitude and willful ineptitude are the secrets to a successful life. Of course they aren't. But there is something to be said for having

the courage of one's convictions, for forging ahead regardless of the opinions or judgments or songs of others,
regardless of their doubts or even of your own. There's
something to be said for these things, and, one day, I
swear, I'm going to say it. In the meantime: Sis Boom
Bah, Cindy, Rah.

Semper Practicalis

"You have a fine fat ass," the man said to me. Or it's what I thought he said. I wasn't sure. The room was very loud and I was standing on a chair. I looked at him and mouthed "What?"

"You have a fine fat ass," he yelled this time.

There were maybe a hundred people dancing in ski boots, some, like myself, standing on chairs or banquettes, screaming the lyrics to "Brown Sugar" or maybe it was "American Pie" or "Freebird" or "Born to Run," all of which were at some point sung by a guy with an acoustic guitar and an amp. Après-ski bar music reached its zenith by the mid-70s and since then there has been a tacit agreement between skiers and local musicians that there has been nothing better since. Even with great music, though, it isn't easy to dance in ski boots. They are heavy and severely restrict movement in your feet and ankles.

You are basically confined to waving your arms, bobbing your head, and wriggling your ass back and forth.

"She has a fine fat ass," he yelled again, this time to our friend Bill, whom perhaps he mistook for the kind of fellow reveler who enjoys it when strange men make obnoxious comments to women in bars.

Or at least that's what we *thought* he said. It also sounded like "She's got a fa fa aah." So we wanted to be sure.

"What did you say?" yelled Bill to the guy.

The guy repeated it: "She's got a fine fat ass!"

Well, would a stranger really say that to me? Was it a compliment or an insult? Is the word *fat,* when preceded by the adjective *fine,* considered a pleasantry? *That's a fine fat ham you've got there* sounds okay. But put it all in front of the word *ass* and, well, there's always a bit of confusion when a stranger uses *ass* in a sentence. It is less alarming than some other things he could say, like *pussy,* but still, a violation. Once, a long time ago, I was in a theater class doing a relaxation exercise. I was lying on the floor, as were my classmates, and the teacher, with whom I had a particularly good rapport, had worked his way around the room to me. In order to encourage me to relax my body even further, he lifted my head gently, and then each of my arms and then legs, and then set them down again. He was checking for a certain heaviness, which is a sign of deep relaxation. He talked me through it, reminding me where tension lurked—in my shoulders and neck, my jaw, my back, my stomach, my hips, my vagina. My what? Yes, the man said "vagina" to me. We had done this many times before, yet he had never, ever said "vagina." I don't care what kind of acting I'm supposed to be doing, I don't need to be reminded to relax my vagina.

Anyway, Bill stood up. David, who was out of earshot, saw Bill get up, so he got up, too. David's relationship to Bill is like some people's to Jesus. He often asks himself, WWBD, or What Would Bill Do, and then he does it, sometimes even if Bill is not there.

What Bill was going to do *now* I didn't know. He isn't exactly imposing; he is a bit under six feet tall, broadshouldered but not strapping, with short blond hair. His face somehow manages to be both rugged and sweet at the same time. He is not easily riled; nor is he spoiling for a fight. But he has a clear, authoritative, manly man voice. Bill leaned in close to the guy and said something that he later claimed was "We don't appreciate that kind of talk," but I'm not so sure. The guy backed away and put up his hands, palms out, in the old-fashioned sign of surrender. Then he looked at me and mumbled what was either an apology or "Hey, sa fa so," and left.

This was maybe twelve or thirteen years ago, and it was one of my earliest experiences of Bill. I have learned that he is the kind of guy who quietly goes around saving people's asses, fine fat or otherwise. Sure, David's pretty solid. He can be depended upon for various sorts of protection and comfort. He is on occasion brave and doesn't become unglued in an emergency. He's my husband and I love him, but Bill possesses a rare ability to spring into action, to see clearly what course must be taken, to galvanize and organize his companions, to keep everyone safe.

I have seen Bill race through a flooded tunnel when, on an early-summer hike across a rain-swollen river, the line leader, a guy named Pat, lost his footing on some slippery concrete and went shooting out the far end into a swirling pool. Bill, who had taken up the rear, flew through the passage and followed Pat into the river. It happened so quickly, Pat flipping off the edge and Bill blazing by me, that I know there could not have been time to formulate a rescue plan. I think a neon light flashed before Bill's eyes, which read, "Pat down; save Pat." I have seen Bill similarly scrambling along the edge of Lake Superior, following the progress of a canoe piloted by David, myself, and another, equally stupid guy on a windy, white-capped, un-canoe-friendly day. Bill stripped in preparation for a lake rescue, despite the fact that the water in Lake Superior is so cold that a person, even a person like Bill, couldn't survive after a couple of minutes in it. Every year he leaps into that lake from a twenty-foot boulder (and so, of course, does David), for kicks. Once, Bill had to be physically restrained so he wouldn't jump off a waterfall after a friend's dog lost its footing.

I have seen Bill do things that no one else had the guts to do, and yet I have never seen him do something reckless. Except for the time when he put an aluminum cooking pot on his head and stood outside in a hail storm. He laughed and laughed as golf ball–sized hailstones pinged off his head and the rest of us watched through the window.

What's the deal with Bill? I finally asked David one day.

His answer: the Marines.

Bill was a Marine for the four years between college and business school, after which he returned to civilian life for good. Bill's late grandfather fought in WWII. His father was in the Marines during the Korean War, and, in fact, still exudes Marine through every pore, like a scent. Unlike Bill, who is loose and easygoing, his father appears upon first impression sinewy and forbidding, efficient, private. His voice is gruff and deep, like Bill's, only more so. When he speaks, dogs behave. He must be around seventy-five, but he is in battle-ready form. From the back, in old jeans and a T-shirt, he might be taken for thirty. Bill's family has a large stone house on the shore of Lake Superior, a couple of hours north of Duluth, kind of a Manderley for the woodsy set. David and I have spent many Fourth of July holidays there, and we always arrived just in time, it seems, to witness

Bill's father engaged in some activity for which a man half his age would not be fit. Pushing wheelbarrows full of rocks, digging tree wells. Once we drove up to find him standing on the limb of a tree, fifteen feet in the air, cutting another limb off with a handsaw. How he got up there and how he got down again I still do not know. He scared the shit out of me when we first met, but that passed; he has a wry sense of humor and an old-fashioned gentility, and now I am sort of inappropriately attracted to him.

And let me say that Bill's mother is no slouch either. She comes from hearty Duluth stock, plays tennis, and hikes across small countries. She is a lovely, genial woman without a mean bone in her body, yet were we to be pitted against one another on an episode of the *World Wrestling Entertainment's Friday Night Smackdown*, she would most likely smack me down.

No Fourth of July weekend at the lake was complete without a group hike. Bill's father would lead roughly twenty people, carrying enough water for everyone in a rucksack on his back. I had come to refer to these hikes as "death marches," and there was no such thing as a pass. If you didn't go with the group, then you couldn't return triumphantly with the group. You couldn't justifiably stuff your face at dinner, or take part in the colorful recounting of the hike experience. One year, maybe it was '97 or '98, before John was born, it was decided that we should go off the barely beaten path and do something Bill's family call bushwhacking. I think I'd heard this term once before, with regard to the country of Australia during the time when it was populated only by English convicts, but to continue, the idea was that we would bushwhack our way through the dense, kudzu-like stalks and branches, and perhaps catch sight of Bill's mother's childhood summerhouse, or the place where it once stood, or something, who knows. Anyway, the bushes we were whacking were very tall and thick and stiff and scratchy and we went on pushing through them for what felt like days and no one seemed to know where exactly we were going, and it occurred to me that any second I might start screaming uncontrollably. Then, suddenly, like out of a dream, Bill's mother appeared, an angel in khaki slacks, a polo shirt, and Tretorns, and led us all to safety.

This is Bill's pedigree. He literally comes from a family of trailblazers. He was born to be a Marine. Wait, I take that back. No one is born to be anything, well, except maybe Pelé and Gandhi. Bill was born to do a lot of things, and for a while, he chose to be a Marine.

Nobody I grew up with, as far as I know, enlisted in the armed forces. Who the heck joined the Marines in the mid-80s? It is easy, when you are lucky enough to be solvent and safe, to take for granted all the things you do not have to do. Work two jobs, for instance. Clean other people's houses. Mine coal. *Enlist.* Obviously plenty of people did, all over the country—the armed forces have great television commercials. My one brush with the military consisted of a fling with a Navy ROTC guy in college. He gave me an engraved bosun's whistle as a gift. One's early experience of the military is not something one has control over. You either grow up in a military family or in a town with a history of enlistment, or you don't. And there are plenty of towns where higher education is more likely than not financed by ROTC programs, or where the military is a way out of whatever it is you want to get out of. It seems, also, that the military knows where to go looking, and liberal, East Coast, upper-middle-class enclaves are probably not worth a recruiter's time. But you don't need me to get on a soapbox. I shouldn't anyway, considering my brother is safely ensconced with a wife and two daughters in Brooklyn and my husband is, well, my husband and not someone else's husband, someone he met at Annapolis or on leave from Camp Pendleton. I am still grateful there wasn't a draft on account of that skirmish in Grenada.

At the age of forty-three, twenty years after he first joined the Marines, two years into the Iraq War, at the height of a successful business career and in the middle of a happy marriage, Bill got himself recommissioned. It wasn't easy. He spent a year filling out paperwork and negotiating a variety of obstacles, not to mention convincing his wife, Lisa, who was vehemently against the war. Amazingly, she supported his decision to serve, while, I imagine, secretly hoping he'd develop some prohibitive condition, like flat feet or color blindness, which was what kept my father out of the Navy. Although, nowadays it's sounding like you'd have to be legally blind or have no feet at all for the military to turn you away.

Initially, Bill was assigned a nice, safe(ish)sounding desk job as an economics officer in a northern Iraqi province, a position that seemed commensurate with his extensive business experience and his interest in nation-building. Unfortunately, another Marine, one less fit for field work, got him bumped from it and now he is a civil affairs officer in Ramadi, the most dangerous destination in Iraq for American soldiers, where the insurgency is destroying the city and has divided its people. Snipers are everywhere and the roads are laced with bombs. Bill is leading a team of Marines on reconstruction projects there. They have been working to set up outposts where Americans can better coordinate efforts with Iraqi politicians and businesspeople, and where Iraqi citizens can receive assistance, air grievances, and be compensated for losses. There are outposts like this throughout Iraq; they have taken longer to come to Ramadi, because every street is a battle zone. It is also Bill's team's job to follow an Army unit on sweeps of enemy hideouts and Iraqi homes and businesses and try to glean information from anyone not shot in the skirmish or arrested. That this seems to be the right job for Bill is not a comfort.

Why did he do it?

Well, he took an oath. *Semper fidelis.* It is a Marine's motto and it means "always faithful." But I don't believe Bill needed an oath to bind him to his obligation. I believe he went to Iraq for the same reason that he stood up for me in the bar, the same reason he dove into the river after Pat, for the same reason he does a lot of things. He did it because somebody had to and he was there at the time. If this sounds overly simplistic, I don't mean it to. I mean rather that it is simple. There are basic points of intervention in a civilized society, and most people know where they are. They are often, if not the majority of the time, easy to ignore, and no one gets hurt. But there are times when it becomes, to quote the writer Joan Didion, a "pragmatic necessity" to act. We can talk about what we believe all we want, but it is in our actions that those beliefs carry weight.

I can't tell you whether Bill believes in the war, whether he thinks it is "right" or "wrong." I can tell you he believes that people need help and that he is capable of giving it. I can tell you that he chose to go to Iraq because he is so fortunate in life as to be able to have the choice. I can tell you he thinks it is unfair that many soldiers serve multiple tours while the rest of us drive around in our SUVs (not me), wearing our smug little peace signs (me).

The word *morality* is much abused in our times. It has become a word people throw out there when they want to end an argument that they cannot win. It has become the clarion call of a gang of bullies, a Machiavellian tool to excuse what cannot be explained. I would like, just for a second, to throw it back where it belongs, to describe a particular combination of common sense and humanity meant, above all else, to ensure not one's personal satisfaction but our mutual survival.

It's a little like ski etiquette. Ski etiquette is the name skiers give to the rules of the mountain. For example, if you knock someone down you don't keep skiing. You stop and check on them and help them gather their equipment, their skis that perhaps have popped off and lie somewhere above or below them on the slope, their hats and poles strewn about in what skiers like to call a yard sale. Another rule is that you don't ski so fast you can't stop when a small child snowplows across your path.

A busy ski slope looks as though all hell has broken loose, it is anarchy, except it's not; people actually, with the exception of a few errant hot dogs and some overly optimistic snowboarders, obey the rules. That everyone doesn't kill each other all the time on the mountain is, to me, a little slice of morality.

The afternoon hours between four and six o'clock at a ski resort might be the jolliest of any in the world. The shared sense of accomplishment, of a day's exertions being over, the warmth of the indoors, the shadows lengthening outside, the music, all these things give you the rare, exquisite feeling that you are in a beer commercial. At any moment the Clydesdales will clop by. The people in these commercials always look so well loved, so unburdened, so fortunate. People at ski resorts actually are, for a time. They spend all day zipping up and down some of the most beautiful mountain ranges in the world, after which there is the après-ski beer and dancing, then hot-tubbing in large communal hot tubs, and dinner with friends in front of a roaring fire in a condo decorated with a moose motif.

This is what our lives were like once in a while. Wishing it back when people are fighting and dying all over the world may seem—no, *is*—the height of self-indulgence, but I do. I wish it back and I will rejoice when it comes, because, above all, it means that Bill is back, too, watching our asses instead of his own.

Mediocre Voyage

When my parents and I arrived at a southern Connecticut hospital at five-thirty A.M. on a humid, hazy summer morning, the only other person at reception had a bullet in his ass. We were there because an x-ray of my lungs, following a persistent bout of bronchitis at the age of twenty-four, had revealed a blight on my internal landscape. It—the blight—was medium to large in size, if you were measuring. If you were thinking *Fantastic Voyage*, it was monstrous. According to a Lung Man, it would have to come out.

I could have feigned surprise at the diagnosis. A thing in my lung! No! But I have to say that somewhere, not very deep in my psyche, I'd been preparing for this day for much of my life. The day upon which I would be pronounced "ill" and become the person at the center of attention I so richly deserved to be.

I'm not sure why some people, i.e., me, grow up with a complex of marginality and some don't. A kind of "everything always happens to everyone else; I wish it would happen to me" mentality. A mentality that does not really distinguish the good things from the bad and for which any attention-getting circumstance will satisfy. Were this bizarre melodramatic wish-fulfillment thing not balanced neatly in my brain by constant, universal dread, I'm sure I would require a serious psychopharmacological solution.

Apropos of all this — at least in *my* mind, which is what "apropos" means — there was a boy named Martin in my high school, who by senior year had lost both parents to cancer. Of course, I had no *actual* desire to lose either of my parents to anything, and yet, and yet, by graduation the orphaned Martin had attained such mythic status that he performed what is now a legendary Janis Joplin imitation from the back deck of our house at my high school graduation party. How these things are connected may be unclear except for the fact that they are. Martin, in my seventeen-year-old eyes, was possessed of a kind of existential freedom. Perhaps he had always had this, long before his parents' illnesses, but it was magnified in contrast to my complete lack thereof. He appeared to me to have shaken something off. Was it fear? The very, very worst had happened, so he need no longer fear its imminence or desire its imagined effects. Maybe that is what it is about for me. Of course, for all

I know, Martin spent much of that terrible year drunk or on drugs or in a manic depression—how else to deal with such a loss, and, also, how else to have the guts, at seventeen, to put on a wig and channel Janis Joplin in front of one's peers? In Connecticut. I have, on occasion, in an exercise of absolute idiocy, brought myself to tears imagining my children crying for me, wailing, really, while I am not there to comfort them, because I am dead. God only knows what Martin must have gone through. But I was, at the time, too naïve or just plain ignorant to know or even conjure any of this. So, in my mind, I wove the threads of loss with those of, I don't know, a kind of glory, and thus produced a fabric that I would finger, like a blankie, for the rest of my life.

I didn't actually think through all of this sitting there in the Lung Man's office, a full year before we found ourselves at the hospital. I'm not that sick in the head— it is just background information, information to explain why as an adult I am dangerously, pathologically empathetic. I am not proud of this, as it is not a good quality. I am not worried about other people so much as it is that their pain triggers a sort of pain in *me*, a jealous pain. It is an embarrassingly egocentric response to the misfortunes of others, the result of a life spent, quite luckily, devoid of any unnatural tragedy. Or maybe it is the lifelong response of a born actress who does not get enough work to satisfy her staggering emotional range.

Where was I? Oh, yes. It turns out the thing in my

lung had been there a while, at least since my last chest x-ray, four years earlier, when I'd had pneumonia. We compared old pictures with new pictures. The Lung Man clipped them all onto a box on the wall and flipped a switch and, voilà, my father saw a side view of my twenty-three-year-old breasts. I pretended not to be mortified, and he pretended not to notice. On a lighter note, I am to this day surprised that my father, who has had his share of x-rays, and who is, more important, both a lover of gadgets and an ardent devotee of the art of self-diagnosis, has never acquired a light box of his own.

We stared at the x-ray for what seemed like too long. The dark splotch loomed menacingly before us. What the hell was it? What did it want? We asked the doctor. He was damned if he knew. It could easily be, he said, one of several things. He then rattled off a too-short list of benign-sounding disorders and recommended a variety of tests to make sure it wasn't anything on a longer list of more serious-sounding disorders. My father and I nodded in agreement, as if, along with *Gourmet Magazine* and *Newsweek*, we had a family subscription to the *J.A.M.A.* But I'm pretty sure all we really heard was that it was either cancer, cancer cancer, or cancer cancer cancer. A few days later, I went with my mother for a C.A.T. scan. The day after that, the doctor left a message on my answering machine, which I called during my lunch hour at drama school, something all acting students do, as though they are expecting a time-sensitive message from Francis Ford Coppola. The doctor suggested a biopsy. Hey, you want to tell my answering machine that I have a yeast infection, fine, but "biopsy" is not really an answering-machine-compatible word.

Our new doctor was not only a Lung Man, but a Prestigious Lung Man. He sent me for an M.R.I. I was injected with a sack of foul liquid and then lay perfectly still in a long tube for twelve days.

Well, I did not have cancer. There, I said it. Whoohoo. I was genuinely relieved. Still, I had a something. I had a P.A.V.M. A pulmonary arteriovenous malformation. A poopidoo-abadingdang-veevee mustiflopolous. No kidding. Who even knew there was such a thing? Who knew you could have a bunch of lousy, congested, good-for-nothing veins sucking oxygen from your bloodstream, like a vacuum cleaner, only to then send your blood on its unsuspecting, oxygen-depleted way? It might have made sense only to my father: when I was young, he used to eat the tops off of cupcakes and put the bottoms back in the package. This is how I understood A.V.M.s at the time. Later, as in during the writing of this essay, I spent several hours researching/procrastinating on the Web, and came up with a more clinically accurate description. "A congenital malformation resulting in direct intrapulmonary connections between the pulmonary arteries and veins without an intervening capillary bed. This causes a right-to-left shunt with peripheral arterial oxygen desaturation. Brain abscesses can develop due to lack of pulmonary capillary filtration of microorganisms" (Michael D'Alessandro, M.D.). Don't feel badly and don't read it a second time. I didn't understand it either.

I also learned that A.V.M.s may occur on multiple sites, including the brain, and their symptoms can mimic migraine headaches—which I get—but you can be asymptomatic, that is, until your A.V.M. bleeds and you stroke out.

Well, at least it's not cancer.

The A.V.M. explained a lot. It explained why I was always out of breath after just one flight of stairs. It explained why, during high school, I could barely run around the field hockey field ten times before practice, a problem which made me appear either out of shape or like I had an attitude problem and, I will always believe, resulted in the election of Susan Starky to co-captain of the girl's field hockey team instead of me. In fact, the whole jogging thing itself had long been a mystery to me. As far as I knew, there was no such thing as a second wind. It was a canard, perpetuated by stringy forty-five-year-old men chasing their youths around the suburban byways and then dropping dead for no reason. "But he *ran*," people would say to each other at the funeral.

I was a decent athlete. I could sprint with the best of

them. I could stop and start and pass and score all you'd want to, but I was not a candidate for cross-country (those weirdos). This should have been clear to me in eighth grade, when I was chosen to represent my home-room class in the Eighth Grade Olympic Pentathlon. We'd had a particularly wimpy group that year and I had been chosen female pentathlete by the time-honored selection process known as The Best of the Worst. I would be expected to compete in the long jump, high jump, shot put, 50-yard hurdles, and 440 dash. I was most concerned about the 440 dash, a single loop around the quarter-mile track that surrounded the football field. Now, I'd already been pretending to jog for a year or so. Running shoes were a fairly new commodity and I'd asked my mother for a pair after I overheard star ath-lete Robby Velos telling other star athlete Tim Franklin that he'd started jogging to supplement his soccer work-outs. Robby and I lived about five miles from each other. Even though I was only able to run two hundred yards in my blue-and-yellow Adidas before I clutched my gut, gasping for air, I still thought there was a fair chance I might run into him.

The Sunday before the Olympics, my good friend Mary Beth, who was hands-down the best female ath-lete in our grade, met me at school and we spent a couple of hours "training." We sat on the grass and talked about other kids and then we jogged slowly around the track in hundred-yard increments. Then we sat on the grass again, drank sodas, and ate snack cakes. Then we jogged a little more. Of course, I was never able to make it all the way around the track but I'd heard that people who trained for marathons only had to be able to run thirteen miles. The other thirteen just sort of, um, came.

Monday morning, the day of the games, I could barely walk. My calves were so tight someone could have plunked out a bluegrass melody on the tendons. Yet I had to don my pentathlon sash and stupid laurel and march in the opening ceremony with the rest of the eighth grade.

When we got to the football field, I was overcome with dread and was right to be. Out of eight female pentathletes, I placed seventh in the shot put, fifth in the hurdles, seventh in the high jump, and sixth in the long jump. I lined up for the 440 in the kind of fear-induced trance I imagined people in the Middle Ages fell into in the moments before they had their heads chopped off. The starting gun sounded and I guess I ran. I kept up with the pack, at first, while ignoring the fire in my calves. But fear of humiliation can only keep you chugging for so long. As we rounded 330, my lungs exploded and I stopped and doubled over. Some friends helped me off the track and I told them I'd stopped because I'd gotten a horrible cramp. I added a limp for emphasis. These days I would have laughed off my incompetence, who gives a shit, really, but back then it was necessary to give it a small martyrish spin, a little drama. Ahh, if only I'd known then that there really *was* something wrong with me.

After my diagnosis, I took myself off to a New York hospital for something called a blood gas. This is a test that measures the level of oxygen saturation in your blood. The blood is drawn from the large vein in your wrist, as opposed to the little blue veins at the inside of your elbow where they usually take blood. This is the vein you cut with a razor when you are trying to kill yourself. It is thick and hard, like a Lucite straw, and it bulges when you make a fist. Don't ever let anyone tell you that this is a painless way to die. Also, never let an intern draw a blood gas. It took my intern an hour and both wrists to get the thing right and it hurt like hell. I walked out with my wrists bandaged and for the next week I looked like Timothy Hutton in the opening scenes of *Ordinary People.*

The results of the blood gas confirmed that if A.V.M.s were like vacuums, I actually had the $900 Miele from the Williams-Sonoma catalog. It was very large and powerful and was literally sucking the air out of me. I'd been functioning for who knows how long with about two-thirds the blood-oxygen saturation of the average person. The thing would definitely have to come out.

How it would do that became the subject of some debate. It was the recommendation of the Prestigious Lung Man that I permit a surgeon to cut open my chest, crack a few inconveniently located ribs, and then excise the offending mass. Under anesthesia, sure, but still. This option required a ten-day hospital stay followed by a six-week recuperation period. That sounded pretty much like the whole summer. My friend Laurie was going on a safari.

We put it off for a little while. We thought maybe another solution would present itself. My parents told their friends. Everyone was very worried. Besides the inconvenience of having no oxygen in your blood, there is the danger of foreign matter floating up through the void to your brain. Blood clots and microorganisms travel through the body to the brain much more easily when there is no, uh, *air* in the way. I didn't really know what the word "abscess" meant, but it was an ugly word, conjuring something fluid-filled and leaky, something grotesque and old-fashioned, like a goiter or a boil.

Finally, a Heart Guy we knew took the films of my naked breasts with him to an Annual Lung and Heart Jamboree in Connecticut and presented them during what I imagine was the light box/soft porn portion of the evening. Afterward, a radiologist named Howard Burke (not his real name!) approached him. A.V.M.s were a pet project of his and he specialized in a nonsurgical approach to them, which resembled angioplasty. It was called embolotherapy and consisted of the placing of a silicon balloon at the entrance to the foul, vampiric mass, thus forcing the blood to reroute — sort of akin to closing all the L.A. exits off the Ventura Highway and compelling motorists to continue along the coast to someplace more reasonable, like Seattle. We called the Prestigious Lung Man and told him to take a hike.

We met with Dr. Burke. According to him, I would be in the hospital two days. Two days? I thought, I don't care if he sucks the thing out through a silly straw if it's only going to take two days. I must admit here that in this regard I did not get the last laugh. I spent the summer waiting tables at a cruddy businessman's lunch joint on Park Avenue South. It escapes me now why I thought this preferable to lounging by the river behind our house in Connecticut waiting for my broken ribs to heal and being catered to/tortured by my parents.

The procedure was to be as follows: I would be sedated with Valium and locally anesthetized in the *groinal* area, so that a small incision could be made through which a catheter could be snaked up the length of my artery. Why we had to enter my artery down *there* when the trouble was way up *here*, at my *lungal* area, was beyond me. Anyway, the catheter was to wend its way up my artery, through my heart, and finally arrive at my right lung, where it would deposit the aforementioned balloon, which would then reside there for all eternity. Compared with major surgery, embolotherapy was considered a safe, painless procedure. The only thing that could go wrong was that during the catheterization, air could be forced into my heart and I could die.

That being said, I'd always wanted to see what the big hoo-ha was over Valium.

I am now of the belief that Valium, taken under the right conditions, might be very soothing. During some stressful occurrence, a co-op interview, for example; or it might come in handy following one of those excruciating phone conversations with your mother, during which neither of you understands a word the other has said and you both become convinced, once again, that you are a changeling. Under the wrong conditions, however, Valium is a poor replacement for general anesthesia. But I'm getting ahead of myself.

Upon my arrival in the radiology wing, I was given two Valium, instructed to undress, and assigned a gurney. I was wheeled into the cath lab, where I was greeted by thirty doctors and fifty nurses, more or less. It seemed to me that the room was awfully crowded for what had been billed a "nonsurgical" procedure. I lay stark naked under a sheet, and a doctor—maybe Dr. Burke, maybe not, they all had masks on—*someone* made an incision and away we went.

Despite the effects of the Valium, I could definitely feel something. A sort of whoosh-whooshing in my chest, as if a little train was zipping around on its tracks. It wasn't that pleasant and I was a little annoyed. I liked the way the Valium felt and I didn't want anything bogeying my high. It's not like I had been expecting the procedure to actually feel good, but I'd definitely been led to believe it wasn't going to feel bad.

Ten minutes or sixteen hours later, the cath lab gang called it a day. In order to track the progress of the catheter, they had been injecting a dye into my bloodstream, something they could only do for so long before it became toxic. And since they did not manage to get a balloon the size of a pinhead through my largest artery within that time frame, they were going to have to try again tomorrow. I was wheeled back to a non-private room that I shared with three other patients, one of whom had just had retinal surgery. She was in excruciating pain. Her son, a very handsome young intern, came to see her. Unfortunately, I've nowhere to go with that.

The cath lab, day two. Everything was the same. I was naked, the doctors wore masks. Oh, for God's sake, I might as well say it: *Story of O*, there, I'm done. Anyway, as Dr. ? prepared to inject a local anesthetic into the other side of my groinal area with a needle the size of a #2 pencil, I realized there was something missing. I was sober as a judge.

"Excuse me," I said to the room, "but I haven't had any Valium."

"They gave it to you upstairs," replied a doctor.

"No, they didn't."

"Sure, they did."

This was an odd exchange. What did he think, I was

hiding the pills in my cheek, like a dog? Maybe I was going to spit them out later behind the blood-pressure monitor or sell them on the street to strung-out med students?

"No, really, they didn't give me the Valium and I'm feeling a little tense," I said diplomatically.

"Well, okay," said the doctor, "but we can't wait for it to start working."

What was that supposed to mean?

A nurse gave me two Valium and then took my hand and said, "Squeeze my fingers." I did, and the guy gave me the anesthetic. I plotted his death, later, in the supply closet.

Once again I was very aware of the catheter's journey along the byways of my anatomy as it sought the right route. It seemed to go in and out and in and out, whoosh-whoosh, whoosh-whoosh, with an occasional, discomfiting scritch-scritch. And, once again, time was passing and not passing. I watched the heart monitor, wondering why they couldn't find room for a little TV set somewhere. Suddenly, I felt a horrible, scrunching, knotty pain in my chest.

"That hurts," I said.

"No, you're all right. This shouldn't hurt," came the reply.

"My chest really hurts a lot," I said again.

"We're not doing anything here that is painful."

Those words weren't out of his mouth before the

heart monitor's glowing mountain range started spiking out of pattern and the regular beep-*beep* of it became *beepbeepbeepbeep*.

Now, I don't know about these people who on the brink of death see their lives flash before them, but I'll tell you what I saw. As I floated above the room, I saw Julie London, who was me but not me, and there was Pernell Roberts and my voice teacher from acting school, Marlene, who had a voice like a fog horn and who did a lot of actors a lot of damage, and she was passing out Bloody Marys with tall, leafy stalks of celery. And there was a film crew from *Nova* and we were all playing Yahtzee! But then I was just myself again and there was an oxygen mask on my face and a nurse telling me to open my mouth so she could put a nitroglycerin pill under my tongue. They'd gotten air in my heart, which feels, I was later told, a little like a heart attack. How inglorious it would have been to die from a painless, non-surgical procedure.

And after all that, they were not able to implant the silicone balloon. They did, however, succeed in blocking off my A.V.M. with a tangle of Teflon coils, which, I was told, would possibly cause me to set off airport security alarms for the rest of my life. I got strep throat in the hospital and spent the next ten days in the excruciating care of my parents.

I didn't get much or really any attention from this whole experience. I wasn't surrounded by a circle of friends, or made love to with particular tenderness by some beautiful, worried boy. I wasn't the beneficiary of a fund-raiser organized by a theater group with whom I'd worked, and nobody painted my apartment while I was gone. In fact, nobody knew anything was wrong with me at all. The whole affair was just too fucking hard to pronounce, much less explain.

My blood oxygen level shot up to normal almost immediately. A few weeks later I ran across Central Park at dusk and then through the city streets for forty minutes as it got darker and darker. I felt suspended in time, no destination in sight, just the cool summer air, the night, and me, running.

The Voyage Continues

If you think it ends there, with me jogging off into the sunset, think again. Fifteen years later I'm writing this essay and doing the aforementioned "research" and I find out that there is now a whole foundation dedicated to the genetic mutation that causes most A.V.M.s. The disorder is called H.H.T., or hereditary hemorrhagic telangectasia (another crowd-pleaser—you can bet I'll tell all of no people about this). I read through the literature and discovered one or two disturbing facts. The first is that at this very moment I may be a ticking bomb.

Evidently it is now customary to screen all of us genetic mutants who have pulmonary A.V.M.s for cerebral ones as well, because we have a fifteen-percent chance of harboring those, too, and when they blow, well, hold on to your hat. Furthermore, *children* of mutants should be screened for A.V.M.s *tout de suite*. Hey, I have children.

I vaguely remembered some instructions from Dr. Burke about having my blood-oxygen level checked every five years, and I believe I had done it after the first five but then, well, you know, busy busy busy. So, I called Burke's office and the first thing he said to me was, "Hey, we've been looking for you." I thought he was being polite, but they actually *were* looking for me. It seems I had fallen off their radar, and everyone knows there's no point in treating a rare genetic disorder if you can't get a decent study out of it.

He was shocked when I told him I'd borne two healthy children, as though he'd expected I'd expulsed two massive A.V.M.s out my twat in their stead, or maybe I'd burst like a balloon from all the blood throbbing through my malformed vessels. After I spoke with him for a bit, it became clear that that last possibility was not so far in left field. A.V.M.s tend to grow during pregnancy, due to increased blood flow, thus diminishing oxygen to the fetus and mother. Egad. He sent me for an immediate C.A.T. scan and we made an appointment for me to bring the results, along with my children, to see him.

This wasn't the first time I'd worried about my children's genetic inheritance. When I was pregnant with Emma, my doctor cooked up some new genetic nightmares to test me for and one day, as I was sitting in his office, about two months along, he informed me in that ultra-speedy/casual way some doctors have of speaking that I am a carrier for a genetic mutation called Fragile X syndrome. Sometimes my ob-gyn speaks so quickly and off-handedly that I'm not even sure he's talking to me. Maybe he's just dictating some quick notes into a small tape recorder in his breast pocket, or maybe he skips every other word in some weird attempt to soften the blow. Whatever the case, I spend the rest of the day thinking I might be going deaf.

Fragile X is the most common cause of inherited mental retardation. A test for it was developed in the early nineties but became standard in New York in the years between my two pregnancies. The only way to find out if the baby I was carrying had the gene as well was to test the amniotic fluid drawn during the amniocentesis. Which was still a month away. It normally takes about two weeks to get the results of an amnio. It would take four more to get the Fragile X results. All told, that's about two and a half months of Fragile X hysteria, the brunt of which David bore, because we'd decided not to tell anyone. I spent days on the Internet, trying to calculate the baby's chances of being retarded. Fragile X is a numbers game wherein the higher the number of repeats of a particular protein-producing string of molecules on this one strand of D.N.A., the greater a chance your child has of being disabled. My child could be normal, a carrier, or somewhere in a broad range of mentally "challenged." My number put me in the carrier range by exactly one repeat. One less and I would be normal (or as close as I'd ever come), and forty-three more and I myself would be retarded.

Both my doctor and the doctor who administered the amnio, and every other doctor I polled during this period reassured me that I had about a one in a million chance of passing on Fragile X to the fetus. But *somebody* has to be the one.

Which is why, in a roundabout way, after speaking with Dr. Burke, I promptly got myself a cerebral M.R.I. and got John one, too, since he has exhibited a few of the H.H.T. signposts—bloody noses and the occasional little burst blood vessel. Emma is symptom-free (and, blessedly, Fragile X–free, as well), and so we will wait and take the genetic test (Another genetic test! Shoot me now!) before we subject her, and us, to an M.R.I. There are few things more unsettling than waiting for the results of a child's brain scan.

It's kind of funny, because I always thought that it would be David who passed down all the unwanted genetic material. I'm just hoping that no more freakazoid mutations turn up. I don't want the drama. Maybe I thought I did once, but I sure as hell don't anymore.

Unfortunately, it seems my children do. Sure, I may not stir up much interest in incomprehensible physiological conditions, but what's to stop them from assuming the mantle of my mental illness? I mean, who doesn't want to be at the center of a medical crisis? Emma, obsessed with Snow White, puts on a Snow White costume (the best forty bucks I ever spent, and the worst, if you know what I mean) in order to—what, belt out "Hi Ho, Hi Ho"? Sweep the dwarfs' adorable cottage with a pretend twig broom? Dance a jig with Dopey? No. None of those. Emma wants, and I quote her, "to fall into a deathlike sleep." She is three years old. She could play any scene from a dozen animated movies, yet she chooses to fall into a coma and be mourned by seven trolls and a gaggle of forest creatures as she lies upon a solid-gold bed. Then she will be awoken by a kiss on the lips from Prince Charming (played by yours truly), who carries her off on a white horse and they live happily ever after. In a castle. The girl has it all worked out. Well, good luck, is what I say. Really. Good fucking luck.

Meanwhile, John's martyr scenario is more psychologically complex and, for better or worse, hews more closely to his mother's script. After several viewings of the Peanuts movie *A Boy Named Charlie Brown* (which, by the way, was made in the 1970s by people who were clearly on acid), John has chosen to reenact, and re-reenact, and, oh, just multiply that by about a thousand, the moment at the beginning of the story, when Charlie Brown is hit in the head by a line drive. Why has he chosen this over being, say, carried home on his classmates' shoulders after winning the class spelling bee? Not for the same reason as Emma; her story, though it takes a dark turn, ends on a high note. John's story, well, let me show you.

Charlie Brown, played by John, and Schroeder, played by David, meet and converse on the pitcher's mound.

"One finger will mean the high straight ball and two fingers will mean the low straight ball." This is what David must say, verbatim. Paraphrasing is not allowed. He must also make the appropriate hand signals.

"What about my curve?" asks John. "And my slider and my knuckle ball? And what about my drop? You forgot about my famous drop ball."

"One finger will mean the high straight ball," says David again, "and two fingers will mean the low straight ball."

Then we pantomime the first pitch, the crack of the bat, and the stunning climax, in which John, who has always shown a gift for pratfalls, flips himself flat on his back, having been beaned in the noggin by the imaginary ball. The rest of us rush to his side, forming a semicircle around his lifeless form, and David, who is now playing Linus, says, "Does anyone know anything about first aid?"

I, as Lucy, respond, "It's probably not serious ... second or third aid will do."

Then comes the moment of Truth, and I mean Truth with a capital T. Or perhaps I just mean the ugly truth, which is that John's Charlie Brown is a chip off the old blockhead. (Ha ha.) He and I are like students in a beginner acting class—and believe me, I should know—in that we only want to perform the most unrelentingly turgid, melodramatic scenes—lots of Inge and Ibsen. It is not John's desire to be lifted out of his martyrdom. He would prefer to maintain it, as I always have, at a low hum. Here's how his story ends. He sits up and groans, "I'm dying and all I hear are insults!"

Luminol

I got an audition for *The Daily Show with Jon Stewart*. It doesn't matter how it happened—a recommendation was made, e-mails were exchanged (were blow jobs in the offing?)—what matters is that it happened. Some people I know in the World of Comedy were of the opinion that I would be an ideal fake news correspondent, and one, whom I shall not name for fear of destroying her reputation, made a call.

Let's take a moment to discuss how big *The Daily Show with Jon Stewart* has become. I believe I read somewhere that it is the most watched news show for people between eighteen and thirty-five, or something like that. Also that it is the most trusted, which should be hard to believe, but these days isn't. It has won nine thousand Emmy awards. It is the apotheosis of comedy gigs for obscure, unknown comic actors and comedians. More people will watch it than will watch your HBO special, that is, should HBO cycle through so many obscure, unknown comedians that they finally come to you.

It looks like more fun than, well, anything.

Since its inception, I have wanted to be on *The Daily Show*. Who doesn't want to be a mock journalist? For me it was right up there with playing Sonya in *Uncle Vanya*.

After the day and time of the audition were arranged, I was e-mailed three old *Daily Show* scripts with instructions to choose and prepare two. They were all hysterically funny, brilliantly written gems, and, unable to choose among them, I spent four days working on all three. This was a mistake. Given a choice of audition material, always, *always* choose right away so you don't waste time. The intensity of my preparation was another mistake. Don't work on anything other than a musical audition or a Shakespeare monologue for more than a couple of hours, which is enough time to make a strong choice about how you want to play it but not long enough to either second-guess your strong choice or beat the thing to death with a stick. This is fine once you have the part, because you have an entire rehearsal period to revive it, but auditions require some spontaneity.

Then I made a third mistake: I decided, since my audition would be taped, to memorize the scripts—all three—as I still had not chosen. Now, there is some research to support this position. The hair on the top of your head is simply not as expressive as your face when reviewed on videotape by directors and producers and such. Still, I have found that if there is one tried-and-true audition maxim, it is that one should not come in with a memorized audition. Know the material well enough to play it without looking down all the time, but don't memorize. Lines you learn quickly and under pressure often elude you when the moment of truth arrives. You will think you know it, and then halfway through the scene draw a blank. Also, you are so worried about the lines you forget to act, or your audition comes off as frozen, as opposed to the brilliant, spontaneous start of a work to be honed later by the director, who will want to take some credit. And there's something else: memorizing, somehow, in the weird, twisted world of auditioning, can come off as amateurish. Certainly, blowing your lines looks bad, but even more than that, working actors don't have time to memorize every audition, they have so many, and they are also probably working on a play or film and are just squeezing this in, so no one is surprised if they just read it a few times and then get up there and let their natural talent shine through.

Now, to be honest, I hadn't seen much of my natural talent lately. Child-rearing and book-writing are time- and energy-consuming endeavors, and leave little opportunity to get a decent haircut, much less pursue one's "dreams." Furthermore, about a year after John was born, my agents dropped me. I know, I know, I'd been saying for the past few years that the agency itself imploded and then disappeared off the face of agency earthdom, that fearful plane which nonactors should be profoundly grateful they know little or nothing of, but it did not do this before it dropped me. It dropped me first. Maybe it was because ten days after John's birth and while I was still sitting on an inflatable doughnut and wearing maxi-pads, I refused an audition for a theatrical spectacular called *De La Guarda*, where all the actors fly around the theater in harnesses attached between their legs. Or maybe they dropped me because I'd made all of $300 for them.

Anyway, when you don't have agents, you don't have regular auditions. Sure you can scrounge a few up, here and there. Student films, fringe festival plays, once in a while people who know your work call you directly—that is, if they remember you're alive. I once cowrote a film partly because it meant I could write myself a nice part.

The main problem with having too few auditions is that each one assumes gargantuan importance. You can't screw it up because it is your only chance to get a job, oh, I don't know, *this year*. In your desperation, you make stupid choices, choices you would *never* make, wouldn't have *time* to make, if you were in the audition groove.

Which, as I said, I was not.

I showed up to the appointed place, the offices of Comedy Central, at the appointed hour, high noon. As I waited to be called in, I alternately scanned my scripts and put them down. Up, down, up, down. I reapplied my lipstick. I took a tiny sip of water and immediately felt like I had to pee, so I went and did that. I returned to the waiting area and it suddenly occurred to me that I should have made up sign-language signals for the whole script and pretended to be doing a simulcast for the deaf. I should have dressed oddly, not in a black blazer and a blue collared shirt, like Samantha Bee, but in lederhosen or a burka, or done it naked, like they do in Canada. I should have rehearsed it in a monotone or a whisper or with a cockney accent. I should have, I should have. My energy, already in the wrong place because I was worried I'd forget the lines I should never have memorized, and because I was *desperate*, became completely unfocused.

There are basically two kinds of adrenaline rushes. One is where it causes all the various working parts of your body to work in sync with your brain, and you might split an atom, if that was a skill you possessed. Clearly, that's not the kind I was having. I was having the other kind of adrenaline rush, the kind that causes the parts of your body to perform independently of each other, with no particular plan in mind, but with enough force to wreck a small trailer park.

The casting director came down a staircase and called my name. We shook hands and I followed her back up. She joked that it was kind of a long way through several halls and that she'd bring me back down afterward. I

searched my overheated engine for a clever response—
step foot in the hallowed chambers that are Comedy
Central and you find you will be unable to speak without trying to make your every utterance a comedy classic. I think I said something like "I could use some crack
right about now." I don't know what made me say it,
I don't even smoke crack, I never have, but I guess I
hoped the word *crack*, in and of itself, would be humor-
ous, which it sometimes is, but this time wasn't. There
was silence and we continued walking. She led me into
a small room with a table on which were copies of the
scripts and some bottles of water. She introduced me to
a young gentleman whose job it was to read Jon Stewart's lines with me while she operated a video camera.
Now, I have done this many, many times—read a scene
with a casting assistant in a nondescript room while the
whole thing is captured on tape. But here I was with my
overworked, memorized lines, carbon-copy correspondent's voice, and awkward crack joke. A ring of sweat
had formed around the waist of my pants, and the audition hadn't even begun.

Astonishingly, the first scene went fine. No problem
with the lines and I thought I got a couple of smiles,
maybe even a laugh. My energy increased several-fold,
my adrenaline pumped, and I became totally unwieldy.
Somehow, instead of just moving on to the second scene,
I found myself telling an amusing personal anecdote. My
mouth just opened and words came out. Piece of advice:

never, I mean *never* tell amusing personal anecdotes at auditions. Nobody cares. Chances are that they've been there for hours and seen God knows what kind of nuts and they just want you to read and then get the hell out. I sat on the other side of the casting room through a week of auditions for my movie and it was very clear what worked. Reading the lines well is what worked. Being a good actor, that worked. People would often ask the director if he had any notes for them and it was all I could do not to blurt out, "Act better." And don't try to be our friend, we already have some.

But I *wanted* to be their friend. I wanted to be *Jon Stewart's* friend, maybe even his second wife. I dreamed about him recently and it was a very nice dream. He seemed to like me a lot. There was definitely a vibe.

So I told some seemingly apropos story and while I was doing that, the word "fuck" fell out of my mouth. Then, before I could stop myself, I said it two more times and said "shit" once. All within the context of the story, but still, I've always had this rule about not swearing during auditions. (That's in addition to the one about no anecdotes, the one about no memorizing, and the one about over-preparing.) For some reason, when you have so little time to make a good impression, swearing sounds unnecessarily harsh and inappropriate. But now *crack* and *fuck* and *shit* were out there and I still had a scene to go. About two-thirds of the way through the second scene, I blew the lines. Since I wasn't holding my script, I had to grapple for the copy sitting on the table, find the lines, and get back to doing them on camera. Instead of continuing on with the script in hand, I put it back down, and one page later blew the lines again. I then uttered "shit" and, soon after, "fuck me." Somehow, in the five minutes I had been in the audition, I had developed Tourette's. When I finished, I said, "Oh, well, what the fuck?" And then I think I said "fuck me" again. I'm surprised I didn't somehow work the word *cunt* in there, I was on such a roll. I imagine the casting director was thinking that she didn't know why I had said I could use some crack when I was so clearly already on it. Red-faced and sweating, I shook everyone's hand, said thank you, and then realized in order to leave I had to follow the casting director back down the hall. At which point I took the opportunity to *explain* my audition.

I left feeling sick and humiliated, like the worst kind of rank amateur. I couldn't reach David or my best friend on the phone. I walked home in a crack daze.

I had not told anyone else about the audition and now vowed I never would. All afternoon I imagined the producer, or even Jon Stewart himself, calling the woman who'd recommended me. First he would regale her with the details of my indignity, after which he would tell his assistant to stop taking her calls. Then my audition tape would circulate the offices of Comedy Central and someone would nickname me the "Crackcaster," or maybe it would air on a worst-audition show, the kind they have for *American Idol.* And then I thought, no, no one would see the tape. It wouldn't make it past the audition room. The casting director would probably just record the next audition right over mine and then forget all about me.

That night, I was scheduled to read an essay I'd written for an anthology at some kind of literary dinner event organized by the sisterhood of a local synagogue. Before we left the apartment, I told David that all I wanted to do was forget about the day. "The dream is dead," I said to him. We would not talk about it that night or any other. No sooner had I lined up at the buffet than David, who, as usual, had been working the room enough for both of us, reported back that one of the other readers was married to a *Daily Show* writer. Well, you can imagine how I felt. I felt as though one shocking humiliation was not enough for the day; I must have another. I accosted this poor man and with virtually no introduction, no prologue or pleasantry, promptly barfed my story all over him. Of course, laughing all the while—ahh ha ha ha, ahh ha ha ha ha. I begged myself to shut up, to no avail. I was completely out of control for the second time that day. I reasoned inanely that he had possibly heard of me already, or was bound to, once he returned to his office at Comedy Central. The best thing I could do was tell him my side. I would turn it into a hilarious anecdote. Maybe he'd go back and tell everyone how funny I really was.

In police forensic work, there is a liquid compound called luminol, which, when combined with blood, glows bluish-green in the dark. It is used to detect traces of blood at the scene of a crime, even if the blood has been visibly washed away. Luminol has entered the popular lexicon in recent years due to the surfeit of dramas based upon police forensics, none of which, might I add, I have appeared on. (I have long been obsessed with *Law & Order* and frankly, given the ubiquity of its various incarnations and the number of actors it requires per show, per season, the fact that I have never been cast is, and there's no other way to put it, an embarrassment.) Nevertheless, I have been enthralled with luminol since 1991, when Valerie Bertinelli played Angela Cimarelli, the sister of a missing woman in the two-part Lifetime movie *In a Child's Name.*

Angela is convinced her brother-in-law has murdered her sister, although up until the final scene of part one, there is still no evidence to support this belief. In that last scene, Angela meets the lead investigator and his forensic team at her sister's house in order to see whether an application of luminol reveals any trace of a crime. When the lights first go out, there is a moment of uncertainty, but then a green glow creeps over Angela's face and those of the investigators. The house is ablaze with chemical reaction. The camera pans across the room to reveal that nearly every surface of the house is phosphorescent. The carpeting and walls and furniture, the stairs, the banister, the upstairs bedroom. It is almost impossible to imagine what Angela's sister must have gone through. Blood was everywhere, *everywhere*, once. And now, thanks to luminol, it's back.

We all have regrets. We all have experiences that plague us, words or deeds we would take back if we could. The memory of some disasters, though, is more galling than others. Blood was spilled that day in the offices of Comedy Central, and it would not be easily washed away. Sure, I could try a special cleanser, I could tear up the carpets, I could leave town, but the evidence is there. Maybe not today, maybe not tomorrow, but *some* day, I will surely run into the *Daily Show* casting director or her assistant on the street, or be seated next to the producer or the writer at a charity function or industry event (I've never been to an industry event but one can hope), and even if not one of them can remember my name, or recall my face, their sheer proximity will set me aglow. Like a latter-day Lady Macbeth, I will look down at my hands and they will blind me with their radiance. Failures are like that; traces remain. Even if we are the only ones who can see them.

I wonder if they are auditioning people for *The Colbert Report*?

The Chronicles of Cynthia

Peter and the Wolf is boring. There, I've said it. It's BORING. My parents are continually trying to foist the thing on my son. I keep telling them to leave him alone. My son has two speeds: Ten and zero. When he is awake he is at ten. When he is asleep he is at zero. He does not have a speed for *Peter and the Wolf.* Perhaps, God forbid, were he in a coma, sort of awake and asleep at the same time, he could tolerate listening to it. Although we would run the risk that he would be trapped in that terrifying middle ground where he could hear the music and the insufferable narration but not be able to ask us to turn it off. And who can stand anthropomorphic music? It is simultaneously coy and pompous. Listen, I'm a bird! Toodle-ee-toodle-ee-too! Bum duh dee dum bum bum, I'm old Grumpa! You can hardly wait for the wolf to kill something.

And, honestly, most people just don't care what a bassoon sounds like. There is maybe one bassoon in a school orchestra, and the kid that plays it often grows up to play it professionally, so no one else has to. I have never, ever, heard a child who, upon listening to a piece of music, any piece, classical, rock, whatever, declare, "Ahh, that was the bassoon." If you want to hear instruments announced as they are played, go listen to part one of Mike Oldfield's *Tubular Bells*, which, if you don't recognize the title, includes the mesmerizing theme from the movie *The Exorcist*. At the end of the almost twenty-minute instrumental, the English comedian Viv Stanshall calls out the name of every instrument Oldfield has played as though each was quite possibly the cure for all of societies ills. Mandolin! Glockenspiel! It's thrilling. *Thrilling.*

It isn't easy for a parent to walk the line between overexposure and neglect. I want my kids to develop sensitivity to art and music, but I don't want to encourage catatonia. There are so many staples of childhood about which it is easy to develop a sort of Stockholm syndrome–like nostalgia. It is crucial to remember the true circumstances of our cultural markers before inflicting them upon our children, even ones that seem to be tailor-made for them, such as *Peter and the Wolf* or, say, the Disney movie *Fantasia*, which seems like it might be a good way to introduce your children to classical music but, in fact, makes an excellent, pediatrician-friendly cure for insomnia. No more mixing bits of Ambien into their milk! Studies have shown that parts of the brain actually do die of boredom. I'm almost sure *The Undersea World of Jacques Cousteau* is why I suck at math.

And while we're on the subject, I'd like to know how many parents are planning on dragging their children, particularly their daughters, to *The Nutcracker Suite* this year. Eight gazillion? And why? The Christmas party it starts with is one of the dullest events I've ever witnessed, surpassed only by the Christmas party I attended in the sprawling Park Avenue family home of a friend from college, where there was nothing to eat but ham and alcohol. And that Nutcracker! It's so fucking ugly. Who believes that a young girl on the brink of womanhood would fantasize about a hideous wooden kitchen tool with a mustache and beard? It's like having a crush on a whisk. Why can't he look like Baryshnikov from the start?

Recently, I chaperoned John's class trip to the Egyptian wing of the Met. Why is it that when schoolchildren visit a museum they are confined to the Egyptian wing or the Native Peoples exhibit? I'm not sure which is worse, wall-to-wall hieroglyphics with no translations or eight hundred arrowheads and five canoes. The star attraction at the Met was not, as you might imagine on this particular outing, the Temple of Dendur, or the many sarcophagi, or the six thousand clay pots. The children, who were five, were most interested in swinging on the rubber-covered chain that surrounded the temple and jumping off the stairs that lead to it. The boys, I must say, showed fleeting interest in the flint knives (you could be the biggest peaceniks in the Western Hemisphere and still your boy-child will become obsessed with deadly weapons) and the girls were willing to give the jewelry a second look (surprise, surprise). Desperate to wring meaning from the visit, I directed John's attention to the abundant statuary and said things like, "What do you think happened to his arm?" and "Wow, where's the rest of him?" and "Hey, he's got no head! Ha ha ha!" A school visit to the Guggenheim, one year later, to view the Kandinsky, Chagall, and Picasso galleries, inspired John to exclaim "Kan-sneezy!" as though he were sneezing. Five months later, it is still a staple of our dinnertime conversation.

On the flip side, one Sunday we were invited as a family to join some friends for a concert given by a group of children's entertainers I'll call the Happy Hippos, who sang original songs and children's standards, dressed in personalized hippo outfits. While I myself have a horror of such enterprises (my brother once called Barney the Antichrist and I have yet to see evidence to the contrary), I decided I should attempt to determine whether I was denying my children exposure to the whole genre of entertainment opportunities that lay at the other end of the spectrum from *Peter and the Wolf* or, say, John's favorite band, Green Day. For over an hour John and Emma and our friends' children sat quietly on the floor in front of the stage while the Happy Hippos performed songs with names like "Ruff Ruff" and "So Long Squeaky," which, if I remember correctly, was a laundry list–like farewell to various and sundry baby toys. I sat in the back singing along, except on each verse, instead of naming the toy, I substituted the word "gun." Afterward, while we waited for our friends to get their Happy Hippo CD signed, we asked the kids what they thought of the show. John looked at us and said glumly, "I don't want to talk about it."

I am sure that early exposure to our cultural institutions is likely to set a precedent for a lifetime of learning, intellectual curiosity, and an appreciation of art and literature and history and science. Well, pretty sure. I am reminded of something my mother used to do. She is a classicist not only in all things pertaining to the arts and education, but in attire, as well. When shopping with me, she occasionally spotted a neat white blouse or pleated skirt or black velvet pantsuit, which she pronounced "good to have." What she meant by this was that it was a wardrobe staple. It would come in handy under the right circumstance. Of course, she was thinking of the circumstances of *her* teenage life, circa 1953: dinner dates at nice restaurants and country clubs, luncheons in the city, the occasional funeral. There should have been some comfort in knowing I was prepared for a variety of events, but it annoyed me just to have these items in my closet. Hmm, what's my point, my point is that children don't need funeral suits. Not yet.

If you grew up in New England, as I did, school trips to Sturbridge Village, a recreation of an eighteenth-century farming village, and Mystic Seaport, a recreation of, that's right, an eighteenth-century seaport, were compulsory. Whether you preferred one over the other depended upon which you thought was a superior snack: saltwater taffy or maple sugar candy. A trek to Mystic usually occurred on a sweltering day in the spring and required much schlepping from one rustic hut to another, where out-of-work actors would make sails of hemp or do scrimshaw. Lethargy set in sometime, oh, around ten A.M. and didn't set out until possibly weeks later. Sure, some kids got a kick out of learning how they get those ships in the bottles or singing a sea chantey to the rhythm of the ship smith's hammer. One day they'll be the billionaire owners of a worldwide shipping conglomerate and I won't. Similarly, the excursion to Sturbridge inevitably took place on the coldest day of the winter, and one year, the village was actually closed by the time we finally arrived, two hours late, in a snowstorm. During the five-hour bus ride home, I somehow ended up sitting next to Christopher Donnelly. That name won't ring a bell with you; in fact, it doesn't with me since I've had to make it up to "protect" the real identity of a kid who hardly knew I was alive. Anyway, we thumb-wrestled and eventually he put his head on my shoulder, a more profound cultural experience than the pewter arts could ever have inspired.

For me, no school outing, however tedious, could compare with a day at the Hayden Planetarium, which inspired a paradoxical combination of squirming and all-system shutdown. The feeling was similar to the one I got sitting naked at my yearly examination by the pediatrician, especially after having reached puberty. After about an hour-and-a-half bus ride from Connecticut, "bus" being a euphemism for a rolling terrarium of adolescent agony, we exploded into the planetarium, scrambling for good seats, knowing that once the lights were down, all bets were off. There were groups from thirty other schools, so actually you were lucky to get a seat next to someone from your state. For the next two hours/ten years, a disembodied voice intoned the interminable story of the birth of the stars and the planets. Back then, Moby did not choose the music. You experienced restless leg syndrome within minutes. You prayed for something to happen, like a fire drill or the destruction of Planet Earth by a meteorite. You fought sleep and lost. There were always a couple of kids who were captivated by the experience, but they were on Quaaludes.

And, of course, not to be overlooked, there were the

trips you took outside of school, trips you took with your family, to Indian reservations in the Everglades, to historical houses in Newport, or national monuments. There was the hazy week in Florida when I thought I didn't need sunscreen—the backs of my legs were so burned that I could not sit down or quite stand up—so my mother figured I would enjoy staggering along behind her on a three-hour tour of Vizcaya, an Italianate villa-turned-museum that was once the home of International Harvester's John Deering. Well, who didn't want to know how John Deering lived? I think it is a good idea for parents to remember that they, too, once stood staring at a roped-off Louis XIV chair and thought to themselves: *Somewhere out there teenagers are playing beach volleyball.*

Occasionally the agony would find you at home, where you thought you were safe. When I was about seven or eight, my mother insisted I read *The Chronicles of Narnia.* Except for *The Lion, the Witch and the Wardrobe,* which had a certain charm—who doesn't want to walk into their closet and not come back—the hours spent reading those books were some of the slowest of my youth. You know how the children go to Narnia for years at a time but when they come back only a few minutes have passed? Well, that's exactly how it was for me. I was in my room each day reading for maybe an hour, tops, but it felt like weeks, even months. The following statement will probably provoke a torrent of hate mail from people who attend yearly Narnia conventions dressed as lions and fauns and dwarves and witches, but I recently reread the books to see if they were as unbearable as I found them as a child and, surprise, they were. All that English dithering, the coy asides to the reader, the unremitting descriptions of the variety of Narnian terrain, the disturbingly reverential treatment of the lion, Aslan.

Who is Aslan? Is he Jesus? Is he the Messiah? He comes and goes at will, making appearances that are years, even centuries apart, sort of like God does now, missing the Holocaust but not Notre Dame football games. Through my whole rereading of *The Chronicles*, I kept hoping a character with the moniker The Old Jew, or Abraham the Israelite, or someone would make an appearance. He doesn't.

The apocalyptic finale staged in book seven, *The Last Battle*, manages somehow to be simultaneously deeply disturbing and painfully dull. Father Time wakes up from a *looooong* sleep, and, at the bidding of Aslan, puts out the stars and the sun. The stars, it turns out, are people, or were once, and they fly through the air and, let's see if I got this right, sort of fall to the earth in burning, sizzling clumps. Horrible lizards and giants devour what is left of the trees and grass and then they themselves lie down and die. Hordes of people and beasts of all races, all species, stream to the threshold of a great magic door, where Aslan greets them. (Yawn. Sorry.)

The faithful are shepherded to Aslan's left, through the gates of a glorious green paradise where their dead friends and relatives from decades and centuries past have been resurrected and await them, and the nonbelievers, swarthy outsiders called the Caloremen (you know what swarthy is code for), as well as most of the dwarfs, giants, and other freaks—pixies, minotaur, and monopods and such—are cast off to Aslan's right, to you know where. It's sort of like *Sophie's Choice*, except that Aslan doesn't seem to mind.

Look, all this doesn't mean that before adulthood I never saw a painting or a cathedral and said "Oooh, aah." But if I am going to be totally honest, it took my *having* a life for me to be interested in anyone else's. And similarly, the lessons I could have used as a child, aside from those that the Department of Education mandated, were ones that were relevant to my life at that time. I needed *cultural* enlightenment less than *sociological*. The weekend my eighth-grade class spent learning about the ways of the early settlers and the Indians (what is it with New Englanders?) at a retreat in Sharon, Connecticut, is a sense-memory only. I cannot recall the recipe for ground-walnut bread or the anatomy of the squirrel we watched some nature guy dissect at the local historical society. What I *do* recall is the melancholy of the late-autumn woods, the pungent scent of the decomposing leaves and graying grass, the bumper car–like energy created by seventy-five fourteen-year-olds in puffy down jackets and rooster hats, none of whom seemed to be bumping off of me.

Perhaps I come off as anti-intellectual, as a reverse snob. (In my defense, I would like to say that, with the obvious exception of *The Chronicles of Narnia*, I spent a good deal of my youth supine upon the various soft surfaces of our house, reading great books — *pretending*, in fact, to be having a life.) But I do believe that there is plenty of time for all this fact-gathering, for lessons and prerequisites. There is a movement afoot in some parts of our country (this part, in particular) to create a race of mini-mes, five-year-olds attired in diminutive versions of adult clothes, who are conversant in several languages and could, were they taller, qualify for jobs as museum docents. Their parents have engaged them in a frenzy of pre-college résumé-building. Sure, some of these children will go to Harvard or wherever and be glad about it, but some will eventually spend *years* peeling off these outer layers in order to discern the person who once was there and had ideas and interests of his or her own. Of course, neither *Peter and the Wolf*, nor *The Nutcracker*, nor Mystic Seaport stands in the way of any child's self-actualization; in fact, I realize that they are meant to *inspire*, yet to my mind all three represent a kind of oppression, a kind of conformity, to which certain children (i.e., me) are susceptible and from which certain children (i.e., me) should have been protected.

Here are some things I remember about my childhood: I remember how once my parents woke me and my brother up at eleven o'clock on a school night because the movie *Ivanhoe* was on. I remember what it felt like to spend an entire day in my bathing suit. I remember how every Sunday, the winter I was thirteen, I played tennis at an indoor bubble with my family, and afterward my father let me drive the car the last half mile down our road.

I remember eating Devil Dogs and drinking orange Fanta with my best friend after field hockey practice, even though we knew dinner was half an hour away. I remember that she and I got drunk together for the first time at a party, freshman year of high school, and how, when I chipped her tooth handing her a bottle of beer, we laughed until we cried. I remember playing TV tag on the front lawn with my brother and his friends on a warm spring night and hoping that something astonishing might happen in the dark. It never did but the hope was exquisite. I remember driving home late with all the windows and the sunroof open, the hot wind drying my clothes, which were wet from secret swims in neighborhood pools. I remember a summer when it seemed like the only song on the radio was "Hotel California."

These are the experiences I most cherish from my childhood, the rare moments when I was flush with a sense of power, with self-determination, with self-acceptance. I want to give my own children the feeling that everything is possible, as opposed to impossible. Open and not closed. I want them to have moments of true freedom. I didn't have a lot of those at school or even at home; I was a good and reliable student and a good and reliable child. The best times for me came on the few occasions when I shook all that off. I knew I could handle all the other stuff, all the books and facts and formulas, the museums and field trips. What I didn't know was if I could do the stuff no one taught you, the stuff you learned by watching, by wandering around, by not worrying what anyone else thought. I want my kids to have the courage to break from the pack. I want them to choose their own cultural markers.

Still, I also wanted to be fair to my son, who, if you ask me, has superior musical abilities. So, one day, during a torrential rainstorm, I walked twenty blocks to Tower Records to buy *Peter and the Wolf.*

Did you know that there are about fifty versions of *Peter and the Wolf*? In my thirty-year absence, the piece has become the classical-music equivalent of *The Vagina Monologues.* Here is a partial list of narrators—at first, unsurprising: Leonard Bernstein, Sir John Gielgud, Cyril Ritchard, Peter Ustinov, and Lina Prokofieva, the composer's wife. But then it starts getting weird: Sophia Loren, Sean Connery, Jack Lemmon, Dame Edna Everidge (Barry Humphries in drag), Patrick Stewart, Sting, David Bowie, Bill Clinton, and Sharon Stone. I saved the best for last: Melissa Joan Hart.

How to choose?!?!

At first I considered buying them all and doing an in-depth analysis of narration styles, even taking into account the orchestra and conductor. Then it occurred to me that this was a neither cost-effective nor efficient use of my time, since it was likely to induce stupefaction. So I quizzed the Tower Records guy, who immediately warned me against the most obvious choices — Bernstein, Gielgud, and Stewart. Too precious, he said. Children don't like to be talked down to. He had enjoyed Dame Edna, but she was, unfortunately, out of stock. We both ixnayed Connery, surmising that perhaps his version, while faithful, might be unintelligible. I love a burr as much as the next gal, but I'm not sure I even understood everything he said all those years ago in *Marni*. It just didn't matter back then, because he looked like something I'd like to eat on a stick, like a popsicle. Anyway, after way too much deliberation, I set off home with David Bowie. He looked great on the CD cover, in a furry wolf hood with ears.

I put it on and we listened to it and John liked it.

Am I disappointed? Was I hoping he'd lapse into a trance or just walk away, disgusted? Maybe a little. But, look, the kid digs anything with wild animals, even *Mutual of Omaha's Wild Kingdom*, which everyone knows is a big snooze fest.

Anyway, *I* was bored.

Some Friendly Advice
for the Man of the House

Okay, so you're dead. Now what? I'll tell you what. In about a year, your wife will be remarried to your son's soccer coach. The one with the English accent. The one who played for the Blackburn Rovers after he graduated Oxford with honors but before he became a self-made millionaire and then retired to mentor young people. He speaks four languages and has a ski house in Alta. He is teaching your children cricket. He and your wife, I mean his wife, have sex all the time, and like Stuart on *L.A. Law*, he knows some sort of secret sexual something or other, a famous move passed down through the hallowed halls of Britain's boarding schools, rescuing generations of pasty, aloof Englishmen from eternal bachelorhood. Except he's not pasty, like Charles; he's ruddy, like Beckham.

Or, *or*, she spent the past year trying to sort out your disastrous business and financial affairs, arguing with your family over the will you wrote in the margin of the Mets' 2003 schedule, and looking for a smaller place, because she can't meet the mortgage payments. Which means she'll probably have to get rid of the dog.

Many women have a widow fantasy. I'd tell you mine except I just did, and it wasn't the one where the dog takes a hike. I'm not proud of it, but, as I said, it's a fantasy, and I guess I just don't see myself as an adulteress. (I can't imagine cheating on him but I can imagine him dead. How sick is that?) The truth is, though, it's never my *real* husband that dies, it's more of an abstract *idea* of a husband. Although once, long ago, we were driving home from a weekend in Vermont, listening to the radio, when we heard news of a terrible plane crash in China. David was due to leave for China that week, and suddenly I became so hysterical that I had to pull over to the side of the road. I sobbed inconsolably for several minutes and then ate two Reese's peanut butter cups and half a Kit Kat.

Preparing for your untimely demise may not seem like a particularly appealing activity, but, to state the obvious, it has gained enormously in popularity since September 11. The war, too, has given it a little boost. If you are one of the happy-go-lucky few who have managed to avoid the subject so far and you have a wife/lover/life partner and kids/dogs/hangers-on, that's fine, it's good to be philosophical about things, but you may want to pull your head out of your ass (you might need some help with this; ask your spouse) just for a moment and take a look at the big picture. Or the small screen. Imagine you're a television character named Jim. You are, needless to say, too young to die, but you just had to play that third set of singles despite the fact that you haven't picked up a racquet since the reign of Bush I. However, this being TV, you don't *really* die. You float around as Invisible Jim, and watch your family get on with their lives. Over the course of the thirteen episodes the network ordered, you overhear your family and friends evaluate your marriage and your character, variously praising and trashing you. And maybe your best still-not-married buddy who's been indispensable through all of this, *as he'd promised,* steps in to take your place. I mean, the kids already think he's a cool dude, and hey, he's pretty sure you'd be glad for them. You're probably smiling down on them right now. Oh, wait, you're not? You're completely freaked out and will spend all of, what, *eternity* wondering whether there had been some undercurrent there all the time, or worse, an over-current?

Season two opens with the episode where the kids decide what to call the new guy. Obviously, if it's "Dad," you're going to have to smite him.

Does David wonder what my life might be like without him? Does he worry? He'd better. I could support myself and maybe half a child on what I make as a writer—that is, if we moved into a *hovel*. Now, I know David's purchased some life insurance, the smarty, hopefully from a reputable outfit, and he has some investments for which I am the beneficiary, or so he claims. He has his own thankless business—Lord knows *I* don't want to have to run it—and as far as I can see, he hasn't left a tract titled *Exit Strategy* on my bedside table, which is worrisome. He has written his will, and I believe I get everything (did I mention that I'd be so so so sad?), although, of course, there's always the chance that, what with all the traveling he does, he has another family stashed somewhere—Shanghai, perhaps. Or, like the architect Louis Kahn, a little closer to home—say, West End Avenue.

But these are piddling, practical concerns. What about the rest of the stuff, stuff like, whom I'd be sleeping with and how soon after? Was that too harsh? I conducted an informal poll of some married male friends, and about half of them were seriously disturbed by the prospect of leaving their wife and kids to their own devices. Not that they didn't trust them—that wasn't it at all. It was more that a kind of existential paranoia surfaced, described best by one of my pollees: "It was like all these years with me were just a diversion from her true course in life—a wrong turn on her journey to soul-matehood. In fact, she is a whole lot happier now than she was with the old husband. Funny sometimes how things turn out for the better, even if they seem tragic at first."

Also among my male friends there seem to be several psychosis-inducing conundrums mucking up the works. There's the "I just want them to be happy, although no one will ever be as good for them as I was" perplexity; the "What I don't know won't hurt me but it still does" paradox; and the "I have a will but I can't remember what it says" confusion. Of course, divorced men (and women) come face-to-face with these issues all the time, but missing from the mix is the extreme grief. It's easier to answer the hard questions when nobody has died. Unless you are unhappily married—then death may come as a relief. If you divorce your wife or she you, you may be bummed out but you'll still see your kids, sooner or later you're going to get laid, and someday you may even fall in love. When you're dead, nuts to you.

I have never even thought about what David's life would be like were I to meet an untimely end. This is partly because for some reason I've assumed that if I go, he's a-goin' with me, and partly because I really can't imagine him with anyone else, he was so lucky to just get me, and I'm no prize. My friend Chris says his wife sees him with the Olsen Twins. Anyway, sometimes, late at night, when I've nothing better to do, I try to envision our orphaned children living with their cousins.

But what if I do bite the big one while David is some-where else, like in the bathroom? How will I want to be remembered? To whom will I leave my children? Just kidding. You know what? I'm not going first. I just decided. It's unthinkable. Well, that's a lie. I think about my death all the time. I just don't think much about *after* my death. I'm all about the dramatic windup. Anyway, the statistics are on my side. So what I say to you guys is this, and really, it goes for everyone: Get wills, for goodness sake, and do the best you can with your finances, whatever they are. If you can afford it, get a little life insurance. If you've hidden investments, unhide them; although, if you're that big a dick, get a divorce and free her up now. Ask your family to be nice to her when you're not around. Don't allocate money for "Lizzy's college" when the children your wife bore are named Scotty and Jane. Don't join your wife's and your best friend's hands as they stand over your deathbed unless you really mean it. Don't leave a letter apologizing for something she doesn't know you did. Don't make a farewell videotape unless you expect to be murdered and want to reveal the identity of your killer.

You can, as one friend has done, make an "ethical will," which is basically a letter to your children in which you express your future hopes for them and impart any sage advice you think they might need—a little like God giving Moses the Ten Commandments. If you can pull this exercise off without expiring from the heartache it will induce, you deserve to live.

Finally, for the love of Mike, get a physical once a

year. Take care of yourself and come home for dinner once in a while. Turn off your Crackberry. Don't be an asshole if you can help it, and let your family know that you love them, on a regular basis, so if, God forbid, your left arm starts to throb ominously during your weekly pick-up basketball game, you'll be comforted in the knowledge that you have been the standard-bearer for all who follow. And who knows who that'll be? Mets third baseman David Wright? Daniel Day Lewis dressed as Hawkeye the adopted Mohican? Could be anyone.

Try not to worry about it, though. What you don't know won't hurt you. Much.

Very Special Thanks

At the end of every book, though mostly first books, and every movie, particularly independent movies, which often rely on the generosity of friends and various and sundry others, there is a list of acknowledgments. Some movies have two lists: *Thanks* and *Special Thanks*. I've even seen *Very Special Thanks*. So many people to thank: families, colleagues, mentors, local businesses.

But not everyone was helpful, were they? Shouldn't there be a list of acknowledgments for detractors, naysayers, underminers? All the people who did not believe in you. The people who got in your way or who tried to bring you down. These people deserve to be acknowledged, too. They should be on lists titled *Fuck You* and *Special Fuck You* and *Very Special Fuck You*. The *Fuck You* list should just consist of people who ignored you entirely. Never returned a phone call and, likely, if they heard your name even now it would not ring a bell. *Special Fuck You* should be reserved for people who are just jerks or maybe never liked you in the first place and are hoping you'll fail. You may not realize this, but probably a third of your friends and acquaintances belong on this list.

The worst offenders, though, recipients of *Very Special Fuck You,* are the people who believed *deeply* in the quality of your work, but whose contribution to your success can be measured in the number of months or years they were able to string not only you but *themselves* along. You see, they love you, genuinely *love* you. Unfortunately, what they love about you *most* is the pretty pretty reflection of themselves they see in you. They have such good taste! They are so benevolent! How good it feels to be so helpful and generous! And superior, let's not forget that! And, lucky *you*! They think you are so talented. With a little hard work and their patronage, it's just a matter of time.

Hopefully, a *lot* of time.

Once upon a time, I got a book deal based upon an op-ed piece I wrote for the *New York Times.* I had not exactly been planning to write a book. I may have thought in passing that one day the various things I was writing would somehow *constitute* a book, but I did not have a book *up my sleeve.* In fact, when I met with the interested publisher, I expected, as it is with many such meetings,

to spend a half hour or so pitching myself as a writer/
actor/humorous person who could possibly make everyone a little money or at least amuse them during office
visits and phone calls. I'd had enough "meetings" in my
long and unillustrious career to know that this was really
what such get-togethers boiled down to, with the agents
turning a crank and me dancing a jig in a red vest and a
fez. To my great surprise, however, it turned out that the
publisher pitched the publishing house to *me*.

What can one say to the offer of a book deal when
one does not even yet have a book over which to deal,
and one is neither a porn star nor a NASCAR driver?

Very Special Thanks!

In the wake of my good fortune, I ran into an old
college acquaintance at a New Year's Eve party. He had
recently moved back to New York from L.A. in order
to take a job at a big public relations firm, but he'd once
worked at a literary agency and, in fact, had represented
some significant authors. He offered his congratulations
and even his gratis personal support. (Would my good
fortune never end?) When we met for lunch the next
week, he had googled some of my published essays and
read them. He loved them, he said, and wanted to foster
my talent and be of help in a mentorish sort of way. He
would send them to important big mouths that he knew,
"big mouths" being a publishing term for people with
big mouths.

I'd always wanted a mentor, to be taken under

someone's wing, to be advised and groomed, introduced around, maybe even to be inappropriately involved with. That's what happened to Alanis Morissette, and look where it got her. This was my first book and I wanted to get it right. I'd take all the help I could get.

My new mentor called often to check in. He told me about his life since college—he had a partner of twelve years (so much for the inappropriate involvement) who was a well-known dramaturge, they had a dog, and they were thinking of buying a farmhouse in Connecticut. We also discussed my writing and the various ways we might go about promoting my book, once it was published. Occasionally he sent me funny letters printed out on heavy, watermarked Crane's stock, using a variety of exotic fonts and hand-decorated with colored markers and rubber stamps. They were beautiful, like modern-day illuminated manuscripts. I must admit I was flattered by this attention, by this obvious desire to interest and amuse me. Once he sent me a bar of homemade soap with some charms floating in it, like fruit in Jell-O—a little animal figurine, maybe an elephant, and a small skull, like the kind with the sunken eyes and cross bones denoting poison and/or pirates.

We continued to meet for lunch at various industry watering holes, discuss my latest essays, and plot my future success. I decided I could, strange soap aside, rely upon his friendship and that my book, when it was ready, would surely benefit from his patronage. When I finished my first draft, I sent it to my editor, my agent, and my mentor.

Everyone seemed happy and excited. My editor made editorial suggestions, as might be expected, and my agent showered me with praise. My mentor, however, was silent. Days, weeks, months went by. Mum from Mentor. As I was preparing to hand in a second draft, a letter came, typed in a single font on ordinary white copy paper that was, in fact, recycled—I saw a lowercase *u* in the top right corner on the back of page one. An omen, surely.

Note: I have added my own, what shall I call them, illuminations.

TO: The Charming and Gifted Cynthia Kaplan

FROM: Mentor

RE: Your Book!

Uh-oh. Everything about this greeting is portentous. The coy yet distancing interoffice-memo layout. The obsequious early use of "Charming and Gifted," capitalized the way people do when they want to be both extra serious and ironic at the same time. The irrelevance of my charm.

What can I say? I worry that you have been sitting up late at night, wringing your hands, quaking in your nighty, wondering "what in God's name could be taking him so long?

Is it SO terrible? Is it UNREADABLE? Has he torn the thing to shreds, and sprinkled the pages into the stinking, murky depths of the Gowanus Canal?" **My mentor does not know me as well as he thinks he does. I have never, ever, imagined anybody doing anything over the Gowanus Canal. I don't even know where the Gowanus Canal is exactly. Gowanus?**

Well, I am sorry if that is indeed the case. Life has been ... ah well, why burden you? **Yes, why?** When I was a literary agent I used to say to my authors who called crying and blah blah blahing when they were late with their books, about their little children or their sick parents or their rent increase or their writer's block, and I'd say, "I'm not remotely interested in the details of your mother's stay at Hazelton or that your spawn was refused entry to Brearley or that your investment in Imclone was devalued when Martha went to jail. I don't want excuses or tales of woe. Just get me your book!" **Oh my God, take your own fucking advice.**

I have been a tad slow getting back to you because your talent, which I think is enormous, demands the utmost care and respect, and in that vein I must admit that, having read your manuscript, you are in grave danger of making an irrevocable mistake. **Four months should be characterized by the words "a tad" only when referring to the Hundred Years' War or the amount of time it takes the light of a dead star to go out.**

Now, if you were the estranged wife of a high profile, drug seeking Major League outfielder, **We're not really going down this road.** or the daughter of a hard partying Hollywood gad-a-bout, **Beep beep.** or if you'd been engaging in secret rendezvous with Newt Gingrich (heaven forfend!) and had a video diary of Newty and some of his GOP buddies doing the electric slide in their Garanimal tighty whities (which we know they wear under their lumpy, ill-fitting worsted wool!) **A parenthetical elbow in my ribs! Ha ha ha!** *I'm going to trash you but we can still laugh!* **Ha ha ha!** then, my dear, you could write whatever you wished. Once the world knows how gifted you are, you could get away with anything. **Even a sucky manuscript! (Heaven forfend!) But, Mentor, what funny, excellent detail. Major League outfielder, Hollywood gadabout, Garanimals. Why don't** *you* **write a book?**

To me and, I'm sure, to your many, many friends, **(Not that many.)** all you have to do is open your mouth and we howl with laughter. Even a mundane "Hi, it's terribly sunny out, isn't it?" is cause for a chuckle. **I suppose I say that with a bit of a British accent, yes?** But my darling, **I'm his darling!** what is the average reader to think? He/she doesn't know you yet, he/she isn't part of your posse **I have a posse!** and I just don't think you can get away with a book of essays or "true stories" as you call them, that do not have an easily identifiable theme. While I know that a true memoir with a proper chronology might stiffle your gift for free association **Do you mean "stifle" or is "stiffle" a term of literary criticism I don't know**? perhaps you could organize your pieces under the umbrella of a shared setting, such as hospitals or nursing homes or some such horrible types of places. Because as it stands, some of your pieces, like the one in which your grandmother vacuums without electricity and feeds her plants cashews, absolutely sing **Tra la la!** while others somehow fall flat. **Truh luh luh.** If this book is just a collection of essays about your life, well, just because I think your life is hysterical doesn't mean the book editor of Richmond Quarterly, Carl Wethersfield and the buyer for the Southwest Independent Booksellers' Cooperative (Sibco **Sibco!**), Jane Fishbein, are holding their breath until your pub date. **What a relief that finally someone, *someone*, has the guts to tell me some hard truths, as opposed to my agent and editor, those lying bitches, who are laying the groundwork for my humiliation.**

Anyway, getting back to what I said, how about organizing the book so people can describe it in a single sentence, like a movie pitch ... "I just read this laugh-out-loud collection of hospital stories!" **Hospital stories! Ha ha ha ha ha ha ha ha!** Or "This season's must-read book is the one about the strange girl and her loony grandmother!" **"Loony" is *so* much funnier than "Alzheimer's." Nice catch!** Now that I'm on the subject, I've been wanting to recommend a book to you. It's by Laura Shaine Cunningham and she lives with her crazy uncles. Is it called *Sleeping Arrange-ments?* I think so. **Oh, I see, so the strange girl should live with the loony grandmother, who, by the way, hardly knows who she is anymore! Sounds like fun!** Anyway, splendid book! **Not like mine!**

Are you mad? **A frown is just a smile turned upside down.** Would you like me to take a running dive off the nearest cliff? **You could walk.** Listen, why don't you have a talk with your publisher and put the whole thing off until you get it right. It's not like the world is biting its nails off in anticipation of your newest tome. **What about my moth-er?** I would hate to see your career start off with a fizzle **That good?** because I believe you deserve so much more, and a ho-hum **Don't strain yourself.** reception to your freshman effort could hurt you later on. Now, if it were up to me, I would fish out the keepers, **Do you want to know what I think you should do with them?** and have you start from scratch, writing a narrative memoir. **Even if it stiffles me?** Of course, it's not up to me, and, ah well, enough said. **Fuck yes.**

Much love anyway- **Save it buddy.**
Mentor **Not anymore.**

Wow. Way to bum me out after the jacket design has been finalized and the galleys are about to come in!

I never saw my mentor again. I did not hear from him after my book was published. Not even a congratulatory e-mail or an apologetic little bar of homemade soap. Still mum, even after all these years.

But that's okay. Life goes on, and I'm not the type to hold a grudge.

Foreign Correspondent

Perhaps it is a result of the astonishing surfeit of survival shows on TV, or the fifteen-year-old holiday card I came across recently, depicting my husband and his buddy Bill in hiking boots and do-rags, astride motorcycles in some remote corner of Thailand, or perhaps it is my secret love for expensive performance outerwear, but it has suddenly occurred to me that I may never have an adventure in a foreign country. I didn't have the guts to do it in college or in my twenties and now that I feel ready it's too late, because I'm saddled with the husband and children I always wanted. And, coincidentally, as if the point needed hammering home, I seem just as suddenly to be finding myself in conversations with people who once lived in a hut at the base of Kilimanjaro, or hiked across Indonesia with only a Nikkormat and a spoon, or thumbed their way through Ireland getting thrown out

of pubs — people who dedicated a reasonable period of
their young adulthood to adventure travel, the upshot
being that their minds are expanded, their bodies possessed of certain intangible but unimpeachable foreign
sense-memories, their photo albums of serious interest.
They are semi-fluent in several languages and have acquired a bevy of international friends and acquaintances
whom they will visit and who will visit them for the rest
of their natural lives. When you talk to them, all their
sentences begin with "I met Dominique in Budapest . . ,"
and end with ". . . so we climbed Machu Picchu."

Some of their adventures were actually altruistic.
These trips were about following the conscience, wherever it took them. I didn't have any of those, either. In
the past three months alone, I have discovered that
friends of mine variously taught elementary school in
the Congo, built bridges in Nicaragua, and gave out eyeglasses to impoverished Mayans. *Their* sentences begin
with "Then, when we were with Médecins Sans Fron-
tières, sorry, that's Doctors Without Borders . . ." and end
with ". . . so that year we spent Christmas handing out
Hershey bars to orphans in Colombia . . . sorry, it's
just . . . (Sob.)"

It has never occurred to me to climb Machu Picchu,
much less join the Peace Corps. Extreme altitudes make
my head ache, and I have a rational fear of rebels armed
with AK-47s. While I have rallied to a number of causes
I believed in, none of those rallies took me beyond a

three-mile radius from my home, unless you count the address on the envelope I put the check in. I've never even worked on a political campaign, stumping around my *own* country, staying up all night to make signs or cold calls, or blow up balloons. I didn't meet my husband at a caucus. I've signed a few petitions in my time, but I never traveled by bus to Washington and stood in the rain on the Mall waiting for Jesse Jackson to speechify or Pete Seeger to sing. I did stand all night in a freezing rain outside Madison Square Garden waiting for Springsteen tickets to go on sale. He sings that old song about war.

Anecdotally speaking—and what other way of speaking is there, really—I have nothing to offer these *buccaneers* in return. Which I resent. What else do humans do besides sit around and tell stories that make them look cool? I've certainly never heard of a *dog* rhapsodizing about a three-year tour teaching English as a second language to children in Mauritius. *(... and by then the flood waters were as high as the tree stumps they use for desks! Woof!)* So, what I usually do, because I don't want to be left out of the conversation, is make a big deal about some little event, tell a grandiose tale of a weekend car-camping or hunting for old doorknobs or some other pointless endeavor. And I put a funny spin on it. *Then there was the time at the party for Bob's seventy-fifth birthday when my hair was attacked by a horde of freaked-out luna moths. Hah hah hah.* Woof.

I am sure it is horrible when the only route out of the ancient ruins is washed away in a mudslide, and one might certainly have second thoughts about one's calling after moving to a third-world country and wearing the same pair of underpants for a week while digging irrigation ditches. But there must be, or they all wouldn't talk about it so much, an enormous sense of accomplishment at having done it, survived it. I've seen the looks of pride on the mud-covered faces in the photographs, the shit-eating grins and sinewy, tanned bodies. (Sound romantic? Does to me!) The wages of sweat equity.

And the wages pay dividends. For years to come, these world-travelers/do-gooders will dine out on their stories, and do-nothings, like me, with neither the experiences nor the tales they inspire, will listen with a mixture of envy and annoyance.

I did not grow up in an adventurous family. We never went camping out West, or sabbaticaled in New Zealand, or walked the Appalachian Trail calling each other by our trail names: Gopher, Birdman, Princess Pine, Cranky Cuss. Neither my brother nor I was sent to live on a kibbutz and harvest olives, which I am not even adventurous enough to like. I grew up in a family where the adventures were, thank God, *tuh tuh tuh,* over by the time my parents were born. *Their* parents had made the arduous trip from the Old World to the New World and that was certainly enough adventure travel as far as everyone was concerned. They had risked their lives for us and now we owed it to them to just stay home and enjoy the fact that we have carpeting.

When my mother finished college, her parents sent her, with two friends, on the grand tour of Europe. All their hotels and flights were arranged in advance. During the day they went to museums and at night to restaurants where they wore white gloves and foreign boys politely asked them to dance. The single story that has endured lo these many years is the one about the evening in Paris, when my mother's best friend, Sugar Silverman, who preferred her hair jet-black, colored the light roots with an eyebrow pencil before going out. She danced all night long with her head nestled on the shoulder of a young Frenchman, and left a large dark splotch on his white dinner jacket.

My legacy.

Unfortunately, my own experience of *la vie Française* lacked something, or, really, everything, of the romance so fondly recalled by my mother. In the winter of my junior year in high school, I lived for a month with a family in France as an exchange student. I was the only student whose correspondent was of the opposite sex, and we didn't exactly bond. He did not find me attractive enough to try to have sex with me and I was obsessed with the fact that he wore the same outfit to school for an entire week. Everyone else became best friends with their hosts and even shared clothes, which, given what I now knew about French habits of dress, seemed inexplicable. Still, the girls walked to school arm in arm, in the French style, and I trailed Jacques by several meters. They were having a different experience than I was, a happy one, a freeing one, and it ignited in them dually an urge to travel and a sense of perhaps belonging somewhere other than Connecticut. Some of them got Eurail passes and spent the summers hopping from city to city, seeing the sights, making friends, and having sex with men with foreign accents. One girl moved to France for the rest of her life. She became an *expat*. In literature, expats always seem to lead groovy, romantic, if slightly seedy, Somerset Maugham lives. They learn the language, eat sweetbreads, shower less often. When this girl came home for the holidays, her conversation was sprinkled with clever little foreign expressions. *Mon cher. Tant pis. Merde.*

What has stayed with me, all these years later, a tiny souvenir of my brief sojourn in France, is Florence. Florence was Jacques's little sister. And while I remember little of her actual personage, and have no particular reminiscences of our relationship, sometimes her name just comes to me, out of nowhere. Not Florence as *we* say it, FLOORence, but Florence in the French way: FloorAHNCE-uh. FloorAHNCE-uh.

Another obstacle to my global emancipation was that sometime in my late teens I developed a fear of flying, which has not diminished with the passage of time. Come on, how is it that we just get on airplanes, la dee da, as though it doesn't require, if we think about it for a *second*, a breath-stopping, life-shortening expense of will to suspend disbelief? And it's not just that I was afraid to travel, I was also afraid to actually *leave*. I was sure that if I left my little life, such as it was, something amazing would go on while I was gone. The life that I had always hoped to live would suddenly start while I wasn't there. Party invitations would come in, men would call for dates, last-minute acting opportunities attended by influential people would materialize. Of course, I stayed home a lot and none of this ever transpired.

In college, when other people were making plans to take a semester abroad, I assumed that if I left for that long, I'd lose all my friends, or they'd become better friends with each other than they were with me, which I think they were anyway. They'd have all these outrageous experiences, urban myth–forming experiences, experiences they'd spend the rest of college reminding each other of and laughing about in front of me. I wasn't just paranoid. All I had to do was go to *sleep*, and life happened without me. One cold winter night, after I'd yawned myself back to my room off campus, four of my friends ventured out in the predawn freeze to paint the front steps of a house on Spruce Street pink and green, a mock tribute to the preppy boys who lived there. This prank became something of a legend that was told and retold for years after. Often people assumed I'd been involved, and I did not dispossess them of this notion.

Strangely, none of the men I know who are husbands and fathers feel the same way—that they missed out on something important, perhaps mind-altering or life-changing, before they settled down. They don't want to be anyplace or anyone other than where and who they are (except, maybe, on a tropical island, divorced, with hair), because they did the big things first. And perhaps they were able to do those things because sperm have the same half-life as a sea turtle, somewhere between eighty years and oblivion. Of course, women, too, go on trips and to graduate school and have careers, but in the back of their minds (and if I'm not talking about you, or you've read any of the three gazillion books recently written on this subject, feel free to skip this part) they are tormented by the presence of a very persistent voice, a *nudge.* The nudge, who might sound a bit like your mother—that's not uncommon—says that it's fine to venture out into the world and make something of yourself, but while you're at it you should get married and stay home and have kids. The nudge understands the desire for freedom but is having a hard time living the dream. And the worst part is that the nudge speaks a modicum of truth: you can't argue with biology.

Now that I actually have, among other things, a husband and two children, meaning, I don't need to hang around trying to *get* them anymore, something quite re-

markable has happened. My fear of mudslides, guerril-
las, etc., has all but disappeared. My fear for my own
safety has been supplanted by my fear for that of my
children. The old worries have been replaced by an entirely new set, wherein windpipe-sized gum balls, nippy
schnauzers, and desperate, childless strangers lurking in
department stores top the list. My body as I have known
it has evaporated into the cosmos and its particles have
been reconfigured and it has returned, postpartum, as
the force field from *Lost in Space*. My job now is to protect my children, not myself, except to the extent that I,
the force field, am obliged to remain alive and well and in
the general vicinity of said children in order to be effec-
tive. Also, or, rather, more to the point, I have begun to
imagine myself to be, in my new, unself-conscious mani-
festation, a buccaneer. Handing out eyeglasses. Joining
that club for polar explorers. Flying on airplanes. As long
as my children are safely on the ground, well, la dee da.

This revelation may account for the feeling I now
have that I've been living in a snow globe. Maybe the
kind with music, sure, but I have been, for most of my
life, happy to look out on the world from the relative
safety of my winter wonderland and gasp with amaze-
ment and admiration at the derring-do of others, at their
selflessness, at the ease with which they have inhabited
the *real* globe. While I wouldn't trade my life right now
for (almost) anyone else's, I'll say this, though it was recently the plot of a failed sitcom: I wish I could take how

far I've come and go back to where I was, just for a little while.

Or perhaps I would simply be gratified by some kind of retroactive inclusion in the occasional anecdote, if once in a while at a social gathering a friend said something like, "Hey, Cin, remember when we were holed up in that lean-to on Rainier?"

Coda

My twentieth high school reunion began auspiciously; I was having a good-hair night, and in the eyes of my former classmates, it seems I had made a reasonable success of my post-adolescent life. I lived in New York City! I was a writer! And an actress! For the first time the popular boys showed some interest. (You'd think twenty years later I'd have stopped caring, but no.) In fact, it appeared that *I* had been the adventurous one. I felt fine, virtually vindicated. A group of us settled with our drinks and hors d'oeuvres at a large round table and everyone but me began reminiscing. I'd heard some of these stories before, and that familiarity, along with my newfound popularity, afforded me a certain license to pretend I'd been more integral to them than I actually had been. Which was not at all. Yet I nodded and laughed along like a pro. I took big slugs of my drink

and mock-choked on it. Ha ha ha ha ha. It was dangerous, I knew, but I was feeling bold, even cocky, and I
thought I could handle it. Which is something drunks
and drug addicts say after they wake up at three in the
morning in a strange city. Anyway, I should have made
a break for the steam table while I had the chance, and
before an ex–soccer player named Chris Cahill posed
the following question:

"Remember when Peg got her head stuck in the railing at McDonald's?"

The place exploded. People could barely speak. Bits
of hors d'oeuvres spewed forth. This event was obviously one of the highlights of my senior year of high
school. The story, such as could be relayed between fits
of coughing and howling was as follows: one autumn
night, after a soccer game against New Milford, a cheerleader named Peg Sealy poked her head through the
wooden railing that separated two booths at McDonald's and got it stuck there.

One of the perks of going to an away game was the
opportunity to have dinner at McDonald's before the
bus ride back to school. If you played field hockey or
girls' basketball, as I did, there was a certain amount
of female camaraderie and bonding at these dinners.
They occasionally turned raucous but, let's face it, all-
girl events where neither drugs nor alcohol were present were not the stuff of legend. (As was, of course,
Kathy Roger's all-girl birthday party where a cardboard

tampon applicator was used as a bong. Memorable!)
If you were a cheerleader, however, every away game
was an actual social event. You traveled on the bus with
the boys' team and then went out to dinner with them
after the game. Furthermore, every game was a party to
which you were required to wear a tight sweater, a very
short skirt, and bobby socks. Amazingly, perhaps inevitably, it came to pass that on game days the cheerleaders
wore their cheerleading outfits to school in the morning.
Never in my life did I attend a party dressed like that,
even on Halloween, when every girl I know dressed like
a whore—not literally, but when my friends dressed as
pirates, they wore eye patches, hot pants, and fishnets.
They were like pirate whores. Or punk whores or flap-
per whores or Native American whores, whatever. The
year of the pirates, junior year of college, I dressed as
a St. Bernard rescue dog. God knows why. Because I
was a fucking idiot, that's why. Anyway, cheerleaders
are just Department of Education–endorsed Halloween
whores.

But I digress. The rest of the evening I spent in a blur.
The giddiness of the Peg Witnesses could not be simu-
lated. I was a good actress, but not that good. Oddly,
the seemingly central question of why Peg Sealy poked
her head through the railing never came up. I realized
this was because it was irrelevant. Maybe she was trying
to talk to some boys at the other table, or just make a
joke, but all these years later, it doesn't matter. What

matters is that I, at this or any other point, would never be in the Time and Place Where Things Happen. I will most probably be stuck forever in the Place Where You Wait and Just Sort of Hope for the Best. Tigers don't change their stripes. Bearing witness to Peg Sealy's imprisonment at the New Milford McDonald's is not the herald of an adventurous life, exactly, but a connection can, and should, be made. You are either in the best yearbook group shots or not. You've either traveled to Bangladesh for the International Red Cross or not. You are either the subject of the story or the unfortunate person who has to hear it over dinner. It began long, long ago and it will probably never end; it has parked itself in the cerebral cortex and erupts, like an aneurism, at regular intervals. Key words set it off: any talk of foreign travel or selfless volunteerism, any anecdote that inspires either knee-slapping or worse, tears. Sometimes the internal hemorrhaging starts spontaneously when I am just sitting around minding my own business, walking on the street, or feeding my children, or shopping for a roll of duct tape. It floods the brain like a mantra: "Remember when Peg got her head stuck in the railing at McDonald's? Remember when Peg got her head stuck in the railing at McDonald's? REMEMBER WHEN PEG GOT HER HEAD STUCK IN THE RAILING AT McDONALD'S?"

So, what to do? While most of my peers lie awake at night conjuring images of larger apartments and luxurious vacations, I fantasize about all of the gritty, dangerous places I've never been and the perilous, character-building things I haven't done. (I even dream about a triumphant return to high school, although clearly it is *way* too late to learn to back-flip off a human pyramid.) And maybe one day, when the kids go to college and I get a divorce, I'll embark on a journey someplace to which jetBlue does not fly. I will get a job as a foreign correspondent, wear hiking boots and a tan vest with many pockets. There will be others of my kind, smart-talking women, and probably, hopefully, men with English accents, and we will sit up at night in foreign hotel bars, drinking whiskey and trading outrageous anecdotes. Oh, the stories I'll tell.

ACKNOWLEDGMENTS

I would like first to thank myself, for writing the book.

Next I would like to thank the magnificent Marjorie Braman and the peerless Amy Rennert. Thank you to the dashing Michael Morrison and the lovely Lisa Gallagher. Thank you to the wondrous Dee Dee DeBartlo. Shout-outs to Richard Aquan and Peggy Hageman and all of William Morrow; they have given me everything I deserve and more.

The following people have helped me enormously: Amanda Green, Kristin Filling, Beth and Eric Berman, Susan Kaplan, Eileen Katz, Chris O'Malley, Jean and Rick Molot, Mason Pettit, Joe Danisi and Stephanie Cannon and Naked Angels, Barbara Jones, Ruth Andrew Ellenson, Autumn Stephens, and David Freeman.

Thanks and love to Alison Fraser and Nat Magee.

To learn more about Rusty Magee's incredible music and comedy, go to www.sweetappreciation.com.

There is no way to properly thank Bill Driscoll and Lisa Hoffman. I bow humbly before them.

Thanks to my dear mother-in-law, Sally Froelich, and to all my brothers and sisters-in-law, Froelich, Moss, and Logan, for their friendship and support.

I literally could not have written a word without the beloved Seeta Seemungal.

In the event that my parents, Sandra and Jack Kaplan, and brother, Steven Kaplan, disown me, I love and thank them anyway. My children are why the book took so long, so no thanks to them. I am going to thank David later, in private.

A NOTE ON THE TYPE

In the late 1350s, while suffering under a repressive fiefdom, French blacksmith Gabriel Cloche-Brulee created a single copy of the alphabet for his young daughter, Clotilde, who could not attend school because one leg was slightly shorter than the other and shoes with lifts had not yet come to their village. For the project, Cloche-Brulee used only a one- by five-inch shred of parchment (which was very expensive in those days), a horse shoe, and the blood-tinged mucous of his pneumocystitic father-in-law. The modern-day version of this type, called Chevalier de Phlegm, has the same curved, footed letter *c* as the original.

Insights,
Interviews
& More...

The Kaplan-Albo Interview

Bill Westmoreland

Writer and performance artist Mike Albo (author of the cult classic Hornito *and coauthor of the insanely funny* The Underminer*) interviews Cynthia Kaplan by e-mail, in an effort to begin what they hope will be the first of many Belles Lettres/Beautiful E-mails, to be published either posthumously, or prehumously, depending.*

MIKE ALBO: *How the hell did you write this book while taking care of your kids?*

CYNTHIA KAPLAN: I wrote the essays very, very slowly, and then when the book was due I think I remember sending my children off to a farm somewhere, the kind to which you send overly rambunctious dogs that you can no longer take care of.

MA: *Your essays, even if they are about the past ("Queechy Girls" in* Why I'm Like This, *your acting* *adventures in your new book) seem like they were written in some eternal "now" . . .*

CK: Actually, there is no "eternal now" that is actually *now*. What you are referring to as my "eternal now" is, in fact, high school. I'm not sure I can explain that. People either get it or not.

MA: *Oh lord, do I ever. Many questions arise after reading this book. I was taking notes while I was reading. One of the notes is "Ask: Is your vagina relaxed?" I can't remember why I would ever ask you this. Please explain, or slap me on the face.*

CK: Once, many years ago, an acting teacher asked me to relax my vagina. Now, I had neither said it was tense, nor, I think, given any indication that was the case. Frankly, I don't know what might have prompted him to think it was, other than that he just wanted to say the word vagina to me. Vagina vagina vagina. It's not so bad. Luckily, though, it was not in front of the class. But since you asked, yes, my vagina is relaxed. Even if I am stressed out, it usually stays pretty mellow. It has its own life to live, I guess, and can't be concerned with my ups and downs. I don't know, maybe it's on valium.

Once in a science class in high school I said the word orgasm instead of organism. *That* was embarrassing.

MA: *Speaking of valium, let me bring up your totally weird and arcane-sounding surgery, of which you write so eloquently in LTBQ (did you noticed that the abbreviation of your book title looks like the name of a gay pride parade banner?). Holy cachongas, that chapter is deeply scary and funny. One question is: Why couldn't you go under—why did you have to be awake while they snaked a tube through your body? And my second question is: Do you have any more painkillers?*

CK: First, let me address what is truly important. Painkillers. Yes, I have some. I always, *always* have Tylenol 3 handy, for migraines or to combat general malaise. Also, not too long ago, I suffered another arcane-sounding illness, pleurisy, which is an inflammation of the lining of the lung. Pleurisy ▶

> " Once in a science class in high school I said the word orgasm instead of organism. *That* was embarrassing. "

The Kaplan-Albo Interview *(continued)*

hurts like a mf-er, and I was prescribed hydrocodone. I never took it, because in my delirium I mistook it for OxyContin, which I'd heard is currently the cause of a heroin-like scourge in Appalachia, or something, and it frightened me, but then my husband used some for relief of pain from a foot injury and he said it was *fantastic.*

Um, what was the other question? Why was I awake? How the hell do I know? Do I look like a doctor? Do I have an M.D. after my name? They kept me awake to freak me out, is the only answer I can come up with.

And yes, *LTBQ* does smack of mixed sexual orientation programming.

MA: *Maybe "Lesbian Transgender Boi Queers" . . . like female to male transsexuals who identify as gay. I actually think this may be a real group out there. You know, I tried OxyContin twice, and both times I just became bitchy. I remember I ran into someone on Commercial Street in Provincetown (of course it was in P-town) and I was totally snippy and pissy to him. Must take a different person. Meaning, your husband has the ability to handle drugs like a Provincetown leather queen.*

OK, next question. I was wondering if there is an update to the life of Bill, the Marine . . .

CK: That's the nicest thing anyone has said about my husband in a long time.

Bill, thankfully, returned home from his tour in Iraq in one piece both physically and psychologically, although on that point, I'm not sure someone who has lived in a war zone speckled every foot or so with explosives ever walks down a dark street again without a serious sense of foreboding.

Last March, Bill and his wife, Lisa, and David and I and a few other friends met out west for four days of skiing. Bill showed us unbelievable, devastating pictures and video of the destruction in Ramadi, and of families and children living in the war zone. Bill won't be going back to Iraq, thankfully, but he is continuing his work with

66 Bill, thankfully, returned home from his tour in Iraq in one piece both physically and psychologically. 99

Marine reconstruction projects in other countries. The guy's a rock star.

And just for the record. My ass is not fat. Never was.

MA: *I would never think of you as an ass-fatted person. Like when I call you up in my mind, I don't think, "Oh, Cindy! That brilliant writer and performer with a fat ass!" I can't believe any one ever did! OK, another thing we have in common: I love skiing. When your book is turned into* Gossip Girl, *you must take me. It's an expensive sport.*

Third thing . . . I have an idea for your next book: expand your chapter on The Daily Show *audition. You offer some of the best advice I have ever heard in terms of auditioning. Like knowing your lines but not knowing them . . . the total inner psychology of standing in those weird office-rooms, trying to emote energy to people who you know are so sick of you and anyone like you and have heard it all and just want you to die, leave, or implode into a tiny dot.*

Do you think there's a book in there?

CK: No. But I think there is a Lifetime Movie of the Week.

MA: *Let's talk about when we first met each other and were performing. Those were some of the first times I was ever on stage. God, I was so nervous. The first piece I ever saw you perform was you in a ski hat talking about your ex-boyfriend. I think you were going to a hockey game or something? Do you remember this at all?*

CK: Yes, that piece was about getting my period on a date to a hockey game with a man who was squeamish about discussing menstruation. Not that I expected him to partake in an evening of conversation on the subject, however; I was just stupid enough at the time to care what he thought. So I overdosed on over-the-counter pain meds. The story ended up in my first book, and was called "World Peace." ▶

The Kaplan-Albo Interview *(continued)*

MA: *Your essay on Rusty, it really lays out all the double ironic humor-music magic that he concocted while on stage . . .*

CK: Rusty was incredible. He would show up with a copy of the *New York Post* and some scribbles on a napkin, and then sit down at the piano in front of two hundred people. Sometimes he would play a lot of doodly nothings for a long time, and we'd all be wondering whether something was actually going to happen or not. Occasionally we got annoyed. One night Rusty sang the date "October 9, 1996" over and over again for about twenty minutes in a kind of musical agony, until, just when we were ready to throw tomatoes at him, he wrapped it up with a lyric about a kid named Jeffrey Maier who had, a day or two earlier, deflected a deep fly ball into the stands during a Yankees-Orioles play-off— a pop fly that otherwise would have been caught by a Baltimore Oriole outfielder, or if not caught, would not have made it over the fence. The ump ruled it a home run, the Orioles lost the game, and ultimately they were knocked out of the play-offs. The Yankees went on to take the series. Anyway, when Rusty sang, "the day Jeffrey Maier caught the ball," the crowd went berserk.

MA: *Wow . . . I'm glad I wasn't there for that one, because I have zero knowledge about baseball, or any sport for that matter, and I would have totally not understood and been so agitated. Sports: I don't ever understand what everyone is screaming about.*

CK: Okay, I'm ready for a really tough question. Go ahead, ask me anything.

MA: *I've got two for you. They don't call me the gay Barbara Walters for nothing! Well, actually, they don't call me that. I don't even know who "they" are.*

(1) **Is there anything in your books that would mortify you if your children read it?**
(2) **You do an artful job of restraint when it comes to bitching about your in-laws, explaining how cohesive they are as a**

❝ One night Rusty sang the date 'October 9, 1996' over and over again for about twenty minutes in a kind of musical agony. ❞

6

family, especially when they vacation. Was this hard to do, or are they really that pleasant and nice?

CK: Mike, they don't call you the gay Barbara Walters because *Barbara Walters* is the gay Barbara Walters. By that I don't mean she is actually gay, but you know, she's kind of gay. And I mean that in the nicest, most complimentary way.

To the questions. If my son read "A Squirrel Stores His Nuts," with all the sex and stuff, he'd be very confused, and probably a little weirded out, since he is only eight. My daughter can't read, so it is not an issue yet. I think that when they are older they might worry about whether David and I ever started having sex again after they were born, and blame themselves (as well they should). And I'll just say this: We did. Very soon after the writing of that essay, in fact. And now it is just bang bang bang, day and night, night and day.

To answer the second question, you've no *idea* what I had to leave out. My in-laws are *insane*. Just total *freaks*. Okay, that is not true. They are very nice and really it is they who put up with me. The worst thing that could be said about them is that they harbor a Republican.

MA: *Do you feel like the personal essay is your medium?*

CK: I've tried to write fiction and, frankly, I stink. Also, my powers of recollection are insufficient for real memoir. I can't remember what someone said to me twenty minutes ago, much less twenty years ago. And the people who claim to remember? They're just making that stuff up.

MA: *Will your next book be a collection of essays as well, or will you switch it up?*

CK: I honestly don't know what the next book will be. Hmm. Maybe I'll just make some stuff up.

MA: *I wish your readers could hear you sing. Your songs are so damn funny. Maybe for the next book you could make a little CD insert?* ▶

> ❝ If my son read 'A Squirrel Stores His Nuts,' with all the sex and stuff, he'd be very confused, and probably a little weirded out, since he is only eight. ❞

The Kaplan-Albo Interview *(continued)*

CK: Well, Mike, I'm so glad you asked! Readers can hear some of my songs on my Web site, www.cynthiakaplan.com, or they can check out the Comedy/Music page for a schedule of my live performances. Then they can come and see me play at a club near them! On the way out, they can purchase my mini CD, *Kaplan v. Christmas*, for only $5.00! That's right, only $5.00!

MA: *I feel such a bond with you because we are both writer-performers.*

CK: You know, I've always been a little hurt that you never asked me to be one of your Dazzle Dancers. I don't know if your readers know about the Dazzle Dancers. Why don't I tell them? People! Mike Albo, writer, performer, Underminer, also has a wicked-cool dance troupe.

MA: *Did you come into writing by way of being onstage?*

CK: I started performing comedy and songs a few years after acting school, while I was still young and poor and performing in badly lit and badly attended off-off-Broadway shows. I'd always written bits and pieces of things I thought were strange or amusing, and then performing just became one more way to get up on stage. And then the writing sort of took over.

MA: *Do you still feel a longing to perform? Or does it interest you less and less?*

CK: What I really would like would be to go back to being an actress for a while, performing someone else's words. I'd like to play all the great roles. Chekhov, Shakespeare, Andrew Lloyd Webber, you name it! I still do a little film work, and comedy in the clubs. But, as you know, I *really* belong on the Great White Way. Perhaps when the Dazzle Dancers go to Broadway.

MA: *Um, perhaps.* ∽

66 What I really would like would be to go back to being an actress for a while, performing someone else's words. 99

Outtakes
"Another Auld Lang Syne" and "Is Anne Lamott God?"

As you may have noticed, my books, all two of them, have been subtitled "True Stories." Actually, I wanted to subtitle this book "More True Stories," or "Son of True Stories," in a nod to the Mad Libs workbooks of my youth. My editor said no. Anyway, my pieces really should be called essays, which is what they are, or at least, what I think they are. They are not really stories, or not just stories, although stories are wonderful— hats off to all story writers—but I write essays. An essay doesn't just tell the story, it tries to illuminate it somehow, to draw a conclusion, to marry a story with an idea. But book publishers don't like the word "essays." Too serious, too academic.

Sometimes, though, when I am writing an essay, the big ideas don't come. Neither do the little ideas, and I wind up with just a story, or worse, an anecdote. I have nothing against anecdotes. Anecdote writing is a skill in itself and hats off to all anecdote writers. But I'm looking for something else.

The piece below, "Another Auld Lang Syne," is one time when I didn't find it. My editor and I actually tried to shoehorn the thing into the book proper, and failed. It is clear why. But one of the great things about the P.S. section is that there is always room for a little something that couldn't find a home anywhere else. Think of it as the movie outtakes that roll during the credits. Or not.

"ANOTHER AULD LANG SYNE"

There I was, stopped at a red light at the intersection where Ford Road meets Weston Road, when a Dan Fogelberg song came on the radio, the one about meeting his old lover in the grocery store. I used to think it was a very romantic song. Just that first line, *Met my old lover in the grocery store, the snow was falling Christmas Eve*, was so intense, so atmospheric—lover, snow, Christmas—that I never noticed how pedestrian the rest of the lyrics were. When I first heard it my senior year of high school it gave me the shivers, and for years, maybe decades ▶

Outtakes *(continued)*

after, every shopping excursion in my hometown held the potential for a fraught encounter—fraught with what, I'm not sure, some kind of retroactive validation, maybe, since I didn't have any lovers in high school. I'm sure I made hundreds of forays to Welch's Hardware and SportMart and the Remarkable Bookshop while secretly acting out the song. I never ran into anybody. There was the time in my early twenties, maybe I was on break from college or drama school, that I simpered into town in a pair of new white shorts on a mission to run into someone or other. After about an hour of pretending to be busy I glanced in a mirror and noticed the crotch of my shorts was stained red. Who knows how long I'd been simultaneously window-shopping and menstruating?

Even now, when I am visiting my parents, I still try to find an excuse to take a ride in the car alone, to ditch my family and drive around town or go slumming on Main Street or at the beach. Sometimes a short trip alone in the car can be like a little vacation for a mother. You can drive with all the windows open, you can blast Radiohead—really, the sky's the limit. And that's just without the kids. Imagine what can be done without the husband. So I leave them all behind, as well as my father, who, like a dog, always seems to want to be taken along, even on the most mundane of errands.

My excuse du jour was that I needed to pick up my friend's ExerSaucer from her mother-in-law's house, where she had stowed it after her daughter had outgrown it. She had agreed to loan it to us for Emma's use. For the uninformed, an ExerSaucer is a helpful piece of baby equipment which, when used correctly, allows the baby's mother to take a short shower.

So there I was, ExerSaucer in trunk, at the intersection of Ford and Weston Roads, singing along with Dan Fogelberg. It was a perfect early summer day. *I stole behind her in the frozen foods, and I touched her on the sleeve*, we sang as I waited for the light to change. It was a long light, a three-way, and somewhere in the middle of the next line, I became aware of raised voices. I looked first at the radio as if it were perhaps jockeying between frequencies, which it was not, and then I looked up

> " I glanced in a mirror and noticed the crotch of my shorts was stained red. Who knows how long I'd been simultaneously window-shopping and menstruating? "

and around. There was no one in sight, only one other car, a convertible to my left, waiting for a green turn arrow. A balding, fifties-ish man sat in the driver's seat and a big-haired, fifties-ish woman faced him from the passenger seat. I stared at them for a few seconds without thinking, meaning, without a sense that I was intruding. The man looked forward while she screamed her head off. Suddenly, they realized they were being watched and simultaneously turned to me. The woman fell silent. I was busted. Or so I thought. Dan Fogelberg sang, compellingly, *We took her groceries to the checkout stand. The food was totaled up and bagged.* The woman then yelled to me at the top of her voice: "HE'S A FUCKING ASSHOLE!" A moment later the light changed and they drove off.

It is hard to describe what I felt then, something close to elation, I think. I felt like a hole had opened in the sky and a ray of universal light had shone down upon me.

Well, I'd gone looking for a fraught encounter and this is the one I got. It has stayed with me—why? I've tried and tried to divine some meaning from it. Perhaps the woman in the car was an oracle, sort of a Ghost of Christmas Yet to Come, sent to remind me to stop obsessing on my past and start attending to my future. But then, I've *already* called David an asshole, although I certainly would love a convertible. Who knows, though, maybe I've got it backwards. Maybe I was there for *her*. She needed validation. We all do. We just never know where we'll find it.

Okay, now here is an idea without a story.

"IS ANNE LAMOTT GOD?"

What kind of ridiculous question is that? I mean, I have already stated categorically that I don't believe in God. And I don't. And believe me, I've read some of Anne Lamott's books and I'm not a fan of all that God talk. And Jesus, well, him too. Really, I've heard just about enough. And furthermore, once, at a wedding reception, with every ounce of courage I could muster—I'm very shy around accomplished people—I introduced myself to her, Anne Lamott, that is, not God, and she completely blew me off. I said, "Hi, I'm Cynthia Kaplan. I'm one of ▶

> " Suddenly, they realized they were being watched and simultaneously turned to me. The woman fell silent. I was busted. "

Outtakes *(continued)*

so-and-so's writers and I just wanted to tell you . . ." and she was carrying a box of plastic bottles of bubbles and wands to pass out so the guests could blow bubbles that would envelope the mountainside in a magical, um, cloud of bubbles, and she cut me off, saying, "I've got bubbles to pass out." Then she brushed by me and left me shamefaced. And yet, Anne Lamott might be God. I mean, if I believed in God, which I don't, but if I did, isn't this what He/She is like? Shows up sometimes, brushes you off sometimes? Like sorry, *busy*?

If you have not read any of Anne Lamott's books, I will tell you what she says. She says forgive yourself. And try to forgive others. And be grateful you're alive, and don't forget other people are too—alive that is—and may need your help staying that way. She says she got all this from God, and that's okay. Just because Joan of Arc heard voices does not negate her bravery on the field of battle. Whatever inspires a person to wisdom and to kindness is fine by me. Let her believe what she wants. In fact, I'm sure she didn't mean to blow me off that day. I am very awkward when I introduce myself, and often choose the most inopportune moments. My desire to overcome my shyness and reach out often inspires a shocking lack of grace. Sometimes I introduce myself but forget to say my name, as though I am so unimportant that a person wouldn't even want to hear me utter the words "Cynthia" or "Kaplan." I have no problem swearing in front of strangers—fuck, shit, fucking shit—anything goes, but say my name, forget it.

And hey, Anne Lamott swears a lot too. She also advocates lying down. I *love* lying down. She gets very, very angry about George Bush. So do I. She has an urge to be mean and terrible and judgmental. I'm all those things. We are so alike, Anne Lamott and I! Which means she probably isn't God. In fact, it would never have occurred to me that she was God in the first place, until she shot me down with that very I'm-too-busy-to-save-you-from-the-infidels-while-I'm-rooting-for-SMU/bubble situation.

I'm going to look into this a bit further and report back. I don't think there is a book in it, though, so if you don't hear anything from me for a while it just means that I've moved on to something, or some*one* else. ∾

> ❝ And yet, Anne Lamott might be God. I mean, if I believed in God, which I don't, but if I did, isn't this what He/She is like? Shows up sometimes, brushes you off sometimes? ❞

Author's Picks
Top Five Essays

May I present to you, for your enjoyment and/or edification, my current desert island top five essays.

"DEATH OF A PIG" BY E. B. WHITE

White's pig falls ill and he, together with his ancient dog Fred, who, it must be noted, seems overly pleased with the pig's ordeal, contemplates the nature of mortality and of personal responsibility. White is a master of the essay. I reread "Death of a Pig" obsessively in the same way my son rereads his first *Hulk* comic book, as though trying to divine some deeper mystery. For John it is an understanding of the duality of good and evil (um, sort of) and for me it is the secret of balancing humor and regret, without cueing the reader when to laugh and when to cry.

Complimentary quote:

Referring to Fred, White wrote, "He never missed a chance to visit the pig with me, and he made many professional calls on his own."

"ON MORALITY" BY JOAN DIDION

In the same anthology as Didion's much more renowned "Goodbye to All That," this essay (to which I referred in "Semper Practicalis"), put into words something I'd been feeling for a very long time, and that is this: It's *not* the thought that counts.

Complimentary quote:

In the wake of a hot, strange night in Death Valley, during which Didion was attempting to write about the idea of "morality" for the *American Scholar*, she mused: "There is some sinister hysteria in the air out there tonight, some hint of the monstrous perversion to which any human idea can come. 'I followed my conscience.' 'I did what I thought was right.' How many madmen have said it and meant it? How many murderers?"

"DINAH, THE CHRISTMAS WHORE" BY DAVID SEDARIS

Sedaris's mother, who emerges as something of a chain-smoking, cocktail-swilling heroine in a ▶

lot of his writing, thrillingly rises to the occasion when her children bring home a hooker. Actually, Sharon Sedaris rises to every occasion, which is one reason Sedaris's collection *Naked* is so satisfying.

Complimentary quote:

When presented with the drunken, lipstick-smeared, rabbit-fur-wearing Dinah, Sharon says, "Oh, thank goodness . . . For a moment there, I was afraid you were one of those damned carolers. I wasn't expecting company so you'll have to excuse the way I look."

"GEORGE WILL VS. NICK HORNBY" BY CHUCK KLOSTERMAN

To Klosterman, soccer is a sport where all of the nonathletes, outcasts, and kids who can't hit a ball or make a free throw and don't really give a shit that they can't, can run around a bit without looking like complete failures. The score is never expected to be much higher than 1–0 or 2–1. They can quit around the ninth grade without apologies and get on with their lives. Which is how Klosterman likes it. But then he discovers that proponents of American youth soccer are trying to put the game on the proverbial American map, and he feels he must defend this last outpost of the outcast.

Complimentary quote:

Klosterman on why Americans will never embrace soccer: "The kind of person who truly loves the notion of sports . . . doesn't want to watch a game that's designed for losers. They're never going to care about a sport where announcers inexplicably celebrate the beauty of missed shots and the strategic glory of repetitive stalemates."

"THE SECRET LIFE OF JAMES THURBER" BY JAMES THURBER

Thurber is the *man*. In this very brief essay, he compares his own prosaic youth with the more fanciful childhood depicted by Dali in *The Secret Life of Salvador Dali*, and remarkably finds some common ground. Attempting to describe it further would be an injustice.

Complimentary quote:

"Senor Dali has the jump on me from the

beginning. He remembers and describes in detail what it was like in the womb. My own earliest memory is of accompanying my father to a polling booth in Columbus, Ohio, where he voted for William McKinley." ❧

Have You Read?
More by Cynthia Kaplan

WHY I'M LIKE THIS: TRUE STORIES

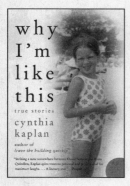

Cynthia Kaplan takes us on a hilarious and sometimes heartbreaking journey through her unique, uncensored world—her bungled romantic encounters and unsung theatrical experiences; her gadget-obsessed father, her pill-popping therapist, and her eccentric grandmothers; her fearless husband, whom she engages in an ongoing battle over which of them is the most **popular** person in their apartment; and, of course, **her vengeful**, power-hungry one-year-old son.

Kaplan's voice is a lot like the one in our heads—the one that most of us are only willing to listen to late at night . . . maybe while locked in a closet. What a relief it is that someone finally admits that she is afraid of nearly everything; that she is jealous even of people whose lives are on the verge of collapse; and that she has, at times, tried to pass for a gentile.

"Funny and poignant."   —*Chicago Sun-Times*

Don't miss the next book by your favorite author. Sign up now for AuthorTracker by visiting www.AuthorTracker.com.